FOCUS ON AFRICA

War and Terrorism in Contemporary Africa

Bridey Heing

Cavendish
Square

New York

Published in 2017 by Cavendish Square Publishing, LLC
243 5th Avenue, Suite 136, New York, NY 10016

Library of Congress Cataloging-in-Publication Data

Names: Heing, Bridey, author.
Title: War and terrorism in contemporary Africa / Bridey Heing.
Other titles: Focus on Africa.
Description: New York : Cavendish Square Publishing, 2017. | Series: Focus on
Africa | Includes bibliographical references and index.
Identifiers: LCCN 2016034407 (print) | LCCN 2016035058 (ebook) |
ISBN 9781502623836 (library bound) | ISBN 9781502623843 (E-book)
Subjects: LCSH: Africa—History—1960- | Terrorism—Africa. |
Africa—Politics and government—1960-
Classification: LCC DT30.5 H445 2017 (print) | LCC DT30.5 (ebook) |
DDC 320.96—dc23
LC record available at https://lccn.loc.gov/2016034407

Editorial Director: David McNamara
Editor: Caitlyn Miller
Copy Editor: Michele Suchomel-Casey
Associate Art Director: Amy Greenan
Designer: Amy Greenan
Production Assistant: Karol Szymczuk
Photo Research: J8 Media

Printed in the United States of America

Contents

South African soldiers have been involved in regional conflicts, but South Africa has been stable and peaceful for most of its very recent history.

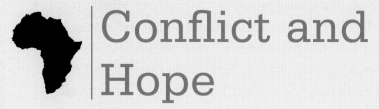

Conflict and Hope

Africa is the second largest continent in the world and has the most countries within its borders. Home to fifty-three recognized countries and a number of disputed territories, Africa has a wide range of political, cultural, and religious norms. While for many African countries these varying views and beliefs can live in harmony, tragic wars have taken place across the continent throughout the twentieth and twenty-first centuries. In the last two decades, terrorism has also become a security issue for countries across Africa, with **non-state actors** establishing strongholds and expanding their influence across the north, west, and east. In this book, we will discuss some of the major conflicts across Africa over the last thirty years, the terrorist threats that have developed on the continent, and what countries are doing to promote peace and stability.

Africa was colonized by European powers until the mid-1900s, with many states fighting wars for independence during the 1950s and 1960s. For states across Africa, colonization was a violent and oppressive experience, and the legacy left behind by colonial powers has led to conflicts across the continent. Multiple leaders have been indicted by international courts for war crimes and crimes against humanity due to actions during conflicts, and mass displacement has created refugee crises in countries across the continent.

Politics and conflict are linked closely across Africa. **Rebellions** and **insurgencies**, as well as disagreements between leadership, have caused wars in South Sudan and Madagascar. In states like Ethiopia and Ivory Coast, political instability and **power vacuums** have brought about ongoing civil war, due in part to the way colonial forces disrupted traditional power structures. In Rwanda and Burundi, the ethnic tensions established by colonial leaders are the origin of **genocide** during the 1990s. In southern Africa, the remnants of colonial governments fueled conflict in Angola and Mozambique for decades, supporting various factions that fought against each other for control of the countries post-independence.

Not all conflicts are rooted in Africa's colonial history. Many have emerged in recent decades as a result of popular protests or opposition to long-standing dictators. In northern Africa, the **Arab Spring** protests of 2011 inspired revolutions in Tunisia, Egypt, and Libya. Today, Libya has descended into a civil war, while Tunisia has transitioned to democracy and Egypt struggles to maintain order. In the Central African Republic and the Democratic Republic of the Congo, rebel forces launched civil wars that unseated the governments and caused prolonged, multiphase conflicts. Separatist struggles in Sudan and Ethiopia were successful, creating South Sudan and Eritrea, but conflict still plagues both young countries.

Terrorist groups have found safe haven against this backdrop of continuous conflict and instability. Terrorism refers to the use of fear and violence to pursue political goals, and in Africa terrorist groups hold various allegiances. Weak governments in Somalia and the Central African Republic are unable to secure their borders or combat terrorist organizations, like al-Shabaab, the Lord's Resistance Army, and Boko Haram. The Sahara region has become a stronghold for various terrorist organizations, including al-Qaeda in the **Maghreb** and Ansar al-Sharia. Libya, consumed by an ongoing war between **militias** and government factions, is home to numerous terrorist organizations, including ISIS and shura councils.

But non-state actors aren't the only ones carrying out terrorism in Africa. State terrorism, or governments using terror to control their countries, is also a concern. In Zimbabwe, dictator Robert Mugabe uses fear and intimidation to maintain his hold on power, and in Sudan the government works with militias to terrorize the people of Darfur.

It's also important to keep in mind that some states can use the label of terrorist against opposition groups, as Egypt's government has long done to **marginalize** the powerful Muslim Brotherhood. Although **Islamist groups** are among the world's best-known terrorist organizations, Islamic political parties are valid and essential members of the political landscape. Similarly, rebel groups are not necessarily terrorists, with some calling for necessary reforms and challenging **authoritarian** regimes. In South Africa, the African National Congress was long considered a terrorist organization and its leader, Nelson Mandela, was labeled a terrorist. But that changed when it became clear that the country's government was violating human rights. Today, Mandela and the ANC are considered heroes in their fight against South Africa's **apartheid** government.

In this book, each chapter focuses on one region as defined by the African Union, discussing the major wars and the terrorist organizations that have emerged in each region. The final chapter discusses the ways African states are working to promote peace and stability, as well as counter the threat of terrorism across the continent.

Egypt has seen a great deal of turmoil in recent years, including a revolution, a military coup, and a rise in terrorist activity.

1 Northern Africa

Northern Africa rests along the Mediterranean Sea in the north, the Atlantic Ocean in the west, and the Middle East in the east. Many of the states in northern Africa are considered part of the Middle East, and conflict in the region is often linked to events in the Middle East. Egypt, Libya, Tunisia, Algeria, and Morocco are all part of both northern Africa and the Middle East, while Mauritania and the Sahrawi Republic are considered part of Africa alone.

War and conflict were common in northern Africa during the twentieth century. The region was the scene of battles and military campaigns during the First and Second World Wars, and wars for independence against European occupying powers took place in Libya and Algeria. Egypt was involved in Arab wars against Israel during the second half the twentieth century, including the Six Day War of 1967 and the Yom Kippur War of 1973. These conflicts shaped the region's international relations, including Egypt's eventual peace treaty with Israel and tension between Algeria and France.

Regional conflict also shaped relations during the twentieth century, particularly between Morocco and Algeria. The Sand War of 1973 and the continued conflict over the Western Sahara have driven the two countries apart, with Morocco leaving the African Union and the closure of the Morocco-Algeria border in response to continued disagreement over the status of the Sahrawi Republic.

Civil war and terrorism have emerged as significant threats to stability in northern Africa during the twenty-first century. The Arab Spring of 2011, which began in Tunisia and spread to Libya and Egypt as well as other Middle Eastern and African states, brought the end of long-standing regimes in the region. This left instability in its wake, with some states establishing strong democratic governments while others, like Libya, have fallen into civil war. Islamist extremist groups, such as al-Qaeda and ISIS (or the Islamic State) have been active in the region, and militias control areas in Libya and the Maghreb.

Recent Wars in Northern Africa

The twenty-first century has seen the end of some long-running conflicts, as well as the beginning of some that continue today. Cross-border conflicts have been rare in recent years, although the insurgency in the Maghreb has drawn in multiple countries in an attempt to reestablish stability in the area.

Algerian Civil War

The Algerian Civil War began in late 1991 and ended in 2002. The war started after national elections were expected to bring the Islamist political party the Islamic Salvation Front (FIS) to power. The National Liberation Front (FLN) had held power since independence from France in 1962, and when faced with an FIS victory, the group responded by cancelling elections. The military, which has long been aligned with the

FLN, stepped in and assumed control of the country. The FIS was banned, and thousands of its members were arrested, which led to the formation of Islamist militias that began carrying out attacks against the government.

The Islamist groups formed themselves into two separate organizations—the Islamic Armed Movement (MIA) in the mountains and the Armed Islamic Group (GIA) in villages and towns. Although originally aligned with one another, GIA was a more hardline organization and eventually began fighting against FIS and MIA when they entered negotiations with the Algerian government in 1994.

Violence hit its peak in 1997, when government forces and Islamist groups are believed to have targeted civilian populations, killing entire villages. In 1999, FLN candidate Abdelaziz Bouteflika was elected president in **uncontested elections**, meaning he did not have any competition. That same year he announced an amnesty plan that would allow militia members to leave their organizations without facing legal action, and violence dropped significantly. Over the next two years, the government fought the remaining members of GIA. The group was effectively broken up, although the splinter group Salafist Group for Preaching and Combat developed into al-Qaeda in the Maghreb. By the time the war ended, estimates put the number of casualties at between 44,000 and 200,000, according to various international and domestic groups. Bouteflika himself has cited around 100,000 deaths caused by the fighting.

Since the war formally ended in 2002, the Algerian government has been controlled by the FLN. The country is largely stable, due in part to its being a **police state** with a **repressive** intelligence service. The government and military maintain close ties, and protests are not tolerated. A state of emergency remained in place until 2011, despite the state's strong hold on power. Algeria has been an active partner in international counterterrorism efforts in neighboring countries, and it has one of the largest armies in the region.

Libyan Civil War

The Libyan Crisis, or the Libyan Civil War, began in 2011, when popular protests forced long-ruling dictator Muammar Gaddafi from power. Gaddafi had ruled the country for more than forty years, taking power in a **coup** in 1969. Under his rule, education and health care were provided by the government, leading to a better quality of life. But Gaddafi was an authoritarian and repressive ruler who did not tolerate **dissent**. He was erratic and unpredictable and supported terrorist activities overseas. His government was accused of human rights violations, and his tight control of power meant that the people had little to no say in how the country was governed.

Public dissatisfaction with Gaddafi's leadership eventually caused mass protests, with thousands taking to the streets first in the city of Benghazi and later across the country to demand Gaddafi's resignation and a new, democratic constitution. In nearby Tunisia and Egypt, such protests (called the Arab Spring) had already resulted in peaceful resignations from long-standing dictators, and many believed the Libyan protests would amount to a similar revolution. But in response to protests, Gaddafi ordered the military to intervene and fight rebel forces and militias, sparking a brutal war that lasted most of 2011.

After Gaddafi was captured and executed, the National Transition Council was declared the legitimate authority in Libya. The group was made up of rebel leaders and had been supported by Western powers and NATO since March 2011. The NTC was only in power until August 2012, but

Libyan rebel groups played a huge role in overthrowing Gaddafi in 2011, but the country has fallen into civil war in the years since.

in that time unrest began to mount. In January 2012, its headquarters were overrun by protestors, and rebel forces began clashing shortly thereafter. By June, areas in the west of Libya were primarily under the control of local militias, and the government struggled to maintain unity.

Following the attack on the United States embassy in Benghazi in September 2012, the Libyan government vowed to crack down on illegal militias. Many of these groups were formed during the uprising against Gaddafi but had since started to agitate for greater **autonomy** and authority over regions of the country. The government gave itself a two-year deadline to disband the groups, but in that time militias grew more active. Some targeted the economy, such as the Petroleum Facilities Guard, which set up a blockade at oil export facilities in August 2013.

In 2014, the conflict erupted as militias began taking over significant cities in the country. The government, formerly located in Benghazi, was forced to relocate to Tobruk when Ansar al-Sharia, an Islamist group that claimed responsibility for the 2012 US embassy attack, took control of the city. Around that time, the Islamist militia alliance Libya Dawn took control of the large former capital, Tripoli, and ISIS established a stronghold along the northern coast. Fighting between rival militia groups forced many to flee, and when an **interim unity government** entered the country in March 2016, it had to do so via boat due to rebel control of the country's airspace.

Today, with the interim government still not approved by all militia groups, Libya has been called a near-failed state. With no strong central government, the country has fallen into chaos. Although some militias are affiliated with Islamist groups, such as al-Qaeda or ISIS, others are organized along tribal lines. Tribalism, or the structuring of society around tribal identity rather than national identity, has further undermined the ability of the interim government to rule due to long-standing tension between the state and tribal authorities. Many fear that the government may be dominated by one tribal group, as has happened in other countries, and all others will be marginalized as they were under Gaddafi.

Libya highlights one of the largest threats to stability in Africa—the power vacuum. In Africa's history, the absence of a strong central government has led to civil wars in states across the continent. In some cases, the lack of a powerful government leads to dictatorship, as so-called strongman leaders take control. But in others, such as Libya, the lack of government can make the country fertile ground for extremism due to the state's inability to provide for the needs of the people. The continued instability in the country has allowed for groups like ISIS to take root in the once largely stable region. While international forces continue to target terrorist strongholds in the country, nearby states have become concerned that unrest could cross the border into Egypt, Tunisia, or southern countries.

Western Sahara Conflict

The Western Sahara rests along the Atlantic coast, bordering Morocco in the north, Algeria along a small border to the east, and Mauritania in the east and south. The area has been disputed since 1973, when the local Polisario Front began fighting against Spanish occupation. In 1975, Morocco **annexed** the area, violating a United Nations call for the area to become an independent nation for the native Sahrawi people.

Until 1991, Morocco fought against the Polisario Front in a prolonged struggle for control of the land. The conflict also pitted Morocco against Algeria; the Polisario Front is supported by the Algerian government, and it's where the exiled Sahrawi Republic government set up its headquarters and refugee camps. Mauritania, which originally fought for control of the area, gave up its claim to the Western Sahara in 1979.

The sixteen-year conflict came to an end when the United Nations brokered a cease-fire between Morocco and the Sahrawi Republic, the government declared by the Polisario Front in 1975. As part of the agreement, the UN required that a referendum be held to decide the future of the area; the Sahrawi Republic is currently recognized only by the African Union and is not considered sovereign by most of the world. But in order for the referendum to be held, Morocco must agree to the terms of the vote. To date, it has not done so

The Polisario Front fought a decades-long war with Morocco over the Western Sahara.

and the area is administered by both Moroccan forces and the Sahrawi Republic.

Although no longer a violent conflict, the lack of change in the status of the Western Sahara continues to strain regional relations. Morocco is the only African nation to refuse to join the African Union, leaving the earlier Organization for African Unity in 1984 when the group recognized the Sahrawi Republic as a state. In addition to fighting the Polisario Front, Morocco was indirectly fighting Algeria, which backed the group. In 1994, Algeria officially closed its border with Morocco when the Moroccan government passed stricter visa requirements for Algerian nationals. Today it is one of the longest closed borders in the world. The conflict has negatively impacted both countries' economies; a study by the World Bank found that both nations' per capita GDP (the total amount of money that a country's population earns divided by the number of citizens) would have almost doubled between 2005 and 2015 if they had worked out a cooperative agreement.

Terrorism in Northern Africa

Since the early 2000s, Islamist extremism has been a destabilizing force in northern Africa. Although some states, like Algeria, have been able to combat terrorism in their own borders, ongoing terrorist activity in the Maghreb and Libya has posed threats to the region as a whole.

ISIS and the Muslim Brotherhood in Egypt

Egypt has seen a rise in terrorist activity since President Hosni Mubarak was unseated in the Arab Spring protests of 2011. That same year, a group then known as Ansar Beit al-Maqdis emerged on the Sinai Peninsula, an Egyptian

Hosni Mubarak ruled Egypt for decades but was forced from power by popular protests during 2011's Arab Spring.

territory that connects it to the Middle East and borders Israel and Gaza. Since then, the group has pledged allegiance to ISIS, and now known as Wilayat Sinai or ISIS-Sinai Province, it has become one of the most active groups in Egypt.

According to a United States State Department report, 2015 saw an increase in both the number of attacks and security challenges in Egypt. ISIS-affiliated groups, like ISIS-SP and a new ISIS group called Misr, or Islamic State-Egypt, are the primary actors in the country. They have carried out numerous attacks against civilian targets, government officials, and foreign nationals. Until 2015, activity was primarily focused in the Sinai area, but attacks have begun outside of Sinai, signaling possible expansion.

Egypt, which shares a border with the tumultuous Gaza Strip, has long struggled with extremism. But the country is also a key example of how the label of "terrorist group" can become political. The Muslim Brotherhood, an Islamist group with a presence in various Middle Eastern countries as well as Egypt, was banned under Hosni Mubarak. The group posed a significant challenge to his rule and drew on its popular support (which stretches back to when it was formed in 1928). Like other groups, the Muslim Brotherhood has a political wing and a **paramilitary** wing, and it was involved in violent conflict with the government during the latter half of the twentieth century.

After Mubarak left office, the group was one of few political parties with significant power. In the first elections held after the revolution, the Muslim Brotherhood won a majority in the parliament and its candidate, Mohammed Morsi, was elected president. But its time in power was short lived, as a popularly supported military coup unseated Morsi in 2013. Since then, the group has been banned from participating in elections and Western countries have moved to label the group a terrorist organization. The Egyptian government has also suggested that the Muslim Brotherhood and ISIS are linked, a connection that has not been supported by evidence and suggests that the government is seeking ways to further marginalize the group.

The Muslim Brotherhood and ISIS, although both Islamist groups with a presence across the Arab world, are very different. ISIS has become known for its brutal tactics and takeover of regions through violence. The threat it poses to not just those in power, but civilian populations and global security in general, has made it a concern for countries around the world. In comparison, the Muslim Brotherhood is powerful because of its widespread public support, which makes it a political challenge to leadership. The Muslim Brotherhood, which has over the years become one of the most active organizations in the Middle East and North Africa, built its base of support through charities that help those in need and by challenging dictators or running for public office, rather than engaging in war to overthrow the government.

The Egyptian government has reason to be concerned about the Muslim Brotherhood, but not because the group could become a terrorist threat. The current government is similar to the government under Hosni Mubarak, with control firmly in the hands of President Abdel Fattah el-Sisi. His government, backed by the military, has cracked down on dissent and protest, arresting journalists and activists. El-Sisi's government has been repressive and violent, and the economy has not rebounded after the 2011 revolution. These circumstances are similar to those that resulted in Hosni Mubarak's resignation. Terrorism, while a very real threat in Egypt, is also a scapegoat allowing el-Sisi to crack down on dissenters and groups that could threaten his hold on power, like the Muslim Brotherhood, in the name of security.

The Shura Councils in Libya

Since ruler Muammar Gaddafi was unseated in 2011, Libya has emerged as a hotbed for terrorist groups, including ISIS. The country has failed to establish a strong central government after years of civil war, and as a result groups like ISIS and Ansar al-Sharia have been able to use the continued insecurity to establish their presence in the country. Although not all militias currently fighting in Libya are aligned with Islamist extremism, Islamist groups are among the most well organized. Many have organized into **coalitions**, pooling their strength to fight the government and each other.

Although ISIS has become well known in the West, it is not the only terrorist group active in Libya. Shura councils have a presence across the country and have been fighting both Libyan forces and ISIS. The two most active branches are the Benghazi Revolutionaries Shura Council

The Islamic State, or ISIS, has become active in Libya in recent years after taking control of the city of Sirte

and the Shura Council of Mujahideen in Darnah. Another shura council group, in Ajdabiya, dissolved in early 2016 when most of its members joined ISIS. Although there is overlap between the groups in Benghazi and Darnah, the most prominent member of both is Ansar al-Sharia, a Salafist group established in 2012. The group is suspected of being involved in the 2012 attack on the United States embassy in Benghazi, an attack that killed the US ambassador.

In Libya, where a unity government has failed to rally support from the numerous militias and organizations in the country, instability has created the perfect conditions for groups like ISIS to establish themselves. The country's borders are weak, allowing for easy crossing from neighboring countries. The airport has been held

The Salafi Movement

In recent years, Salafism has emerged as one of the most prominent movements in Islam. It has spread across the Middle East, Africa, and Europe, and some followers have carried out attacks around the world. Based in Sunni Islam, Salafist thought emerged one hundred years ago and has since become a loosely affiliated group of people who want to return to a "purer" form of Islam. With no leader or unifying ideology, Salafism is interpreted in varied ways by followers, although all adhere to conservative Islamic teachings. Salafist teachings emphasize the importance of emulating the life of the Prophet Mohammed and support sharia law based in Islamic teachings. The movement is considered fundamentalist, with strict guidelines on clothing and other personal matters. Despite its tightly focused vision of Islam, there are still disagreements on legal matters, the place of Salafists in government, and other issues.

Salafism is very conservative, giving rise to a number of prominent Salafist Islamist extremist groups, such as Ansar al-Sharia. ISIS is also affiliated with Salafism, while al-Qaeda's Wahhabi roots draw from far-right Salafism. But these extremist ties, called Salafi Jihad, are just one manifestation of Salafism. Many Salafists are peaceful and opposed to terrorism. Many, called purists, are nonpolitical, although in the aftermath of the Arab Spring some became involved in local political activism and government. Although Jihadists are a minority, those groups have come to define Salafism in the public eye, and Salafist populations around the world face harsh representation and intense scrutiny.

by militias and terrorist organizations, military bases have been attacked and stores of weapons stolen, and the country has become a magnet for fighters, with an estimated five thousand there in 2015. The instability and near constant fighting have also contributed to the global refugee crisis, with the Libyan coast becoming a key area in the illegal human smuggling industry, taking refugees and migrants to Europe across the Mediterranean.

The Maghreb Insurgency

Although Morocco, Algeria, and Mauritania have been largely stable in recent years, in 2002 the states joined other African countries in fighting an Islamist insurgency in the Maghreb. The Maghreb includes all northern African states except for Egypt, although the fighting has included Mali, Niger, Ivory Coast, and overseas forces. Centered on the massive Sahara Desert, terrorist organizations and militias are able to use the largely remote and unpopulated desert as a safe haven, and the neglected borders of the area make it easy for them to travel across state lines.

Many Islamist groups are involved in the fighting, but one of the primary groups is al-Qaeda in the Islamic Maghreb. The group was founded as an anti-Algerian government militia in 1998 under the name the Salafist Group for Preaching and Combat. When the Algerian Civil War ended in 2002, the group continued fighting and carrying out attacks against civilians. In 2005, its leader called for members to accept amnesty from the Algerian government, signaling a possible end to the conflict. But in 2007, the remaining members of the group began working with al-Qaeda under the name al-Qaeda in the Islamic Maghreb (or AQIM). The group, which is the strongest in

Sayyid Qutb

Sayyid Qutb was an Egyptian writer and philosopher who wrote extensively on the political and social role of Islam. He was a leader in the Muslim Brotherhood in the 1950s and 1960s, serving as editor in chief of its weekly newsletter, working on propaganda, and eventually serving on the guidance council. His teachings, which were rooted in an anti-Western interpretation of Islam, are considered the foundation of today's anti-US and anti-Western strains of Muslim thought, ranging from the Muslim Brotherhood to al-Qaeda.

Qutb advocated a vision of Islam that worked against Western influence and emphasized traditional, conservative values. He supported sharia law based in Islamic teachings, with **clerical** leaders running the state. He also argued against democracy as an Islamic value, something that had long been considered part of Islamic political culture. His writings, including his manifesto of sorts *In the Shade of the Quran*, are still widely published across the world. His brother, Muhammad Qutb, left Egypt to teach in Saudi Arabia, where he spent time with Osama bin Laden, who went on to lead al-Qaeda. The infamous terrorist leader was inspired in part by Qutb's teachings, particularly his belief that Muslims must fight against Western culture, which he called *jahiliyya*, or "ignorance." Other groups, including Islamic Jihad, were also inspired by Qutb's teachings. But many of his followers do not see his teachings as compatible with violent extremism, arguing that the killing of innocent civilians would not align with his views.

the conflict, receives most of its money from ransoms paid by organizations and foreign governments in exchange for hostages taken by the group.

AQIM is not the only group active in the conflict. ISIS and allies Wilayat Algeria have a presence, as well as Moroccan and Tunisian Islamist groups. The AQIM offshoot Movement for Oneness and Jihad in West Africa has also emerged, with a stated goal of fighting in western Africa. The group has also formed an alliance with the Tuareg and Mali Masked Men Brigade, calling themselves al-Mourabitoun. All of these groups have been involved in attacks on governments, militaries, and civilians, including foreign nationals.

Regional military cooperation is a key step in ensuring stability in Africa. Here, soldiers from western Africa prepare a checkpoint.

Western Africa

2

Western Africa rests along the Atlantic Ocean and the Cape of Guinea and along the southern half of the Sahara Desert. It includes Benin, Burkina Faso, Cabo Verde, Ivory Coast, the Gambia, Ghana, Guinea, Guinea Bissau, Liberia, Mali, Niger, Nigeria, Senegal, Sierra Leone, and Togo.

Unrest has been common in western Africa since independence, with numerous civil conflicts and rebellions. Some states, such as the island nation of Cabo Verde, have emerged as stable and peaceful states. But others, such as Ivory Coast and Liberia, have struggled with multiple civil wars in the late twentieth and early twenty-first centuries. Rebellions, including insurgencies led by ethnic and tribal groups, have also posed security issues for western African states. Political and ethnic violence has also been an issue in western Africa, including in Guinea where clashes in 2013 killed nine and injured more than two hundred.

In western Africa, conflict and terrorism are not as closely linked as they are in northern Africa. Although many conflicts have erupted due to the presence of terrorist organizations, including Boko Haram in Nigeria, not all of today's fighting is linked to terrorist threats. But in Mali, the

Tuareg, a **nomadic** population, began what is now called the Northern Mali Conflict by fighting for an independent state. Although Islamist terrorist groups are present in the conflict, it is important to differentiate between legitimate forces challenging the government and terrorist organizations.

Although wars between countries in western Africa have been few and far between in the twentieth and twenty-first centuries, cross-border fighting has been an issue. The Maghreb Insurgency, which stretches across western Africa and northern Africa, has become a growing concern as Islamist militant groups have become more and more numerous in the Sahara region. It has made allies of neighboring countries, such as Niger and Mali, as well as northern African states like Morocco.

Major Wars in Western Africa

Western Africa has seen a large number of civil wars and internal conflicts in recent years. Ongoing conflicts are also common, with some moving through several different phases of activity and peace. Some, including the Northern Mali Conflict and the Nigerian Conflict, have continued for more than a decade.

Ivorian Civil Wars

Ivory Coast, along the Cape of Guinea, has seen two civil wars since 2000. The first, which began in 2002 and ended in 2007, split the country in two between warring Muslim and Christian factions. The second, which began in 2010 and ended in 2011, ended when the United Nations and France intervened militarily after thousands were killed in fighting.

The first Ivorian Civil War was the result of tensions that had been simmering in Ivory Coast since 1993, when the president of thirty-three years stepped down and democratic elections were put in place. Tensions along economic and ethnic lines became more strongly pronounced, with an economic downturn leading to conflict between political and cultural groups. Discrimination against foreign nationals, many of whom had lived in Ivory Coast for years and made up around 25 percent of the population, also posed challenges as the country grappled with how to hold elections and whom to allow to run for office.

In 2000, just ahead of a presidential election, a law was quickly introduced and approved via referendum that banned candidates who did not have parents born in Ivory Coast. The law barred Alassane Ouattara, from northern Ivory Coast, from the race. Laurent Gbagbo won the election, although supporters of Ouattara contested, or protested, the election due to his exclusion. Two years later, northern forces rose against the government, effectively taking control of the north. The uprising split the country in two, with Ouattara ruling in the north and Gbagbo ruling in the south.

The conflict was rooted in questions about who is an Ivorian citizen and who has the right to run for office. In the immigrant and migrant worker communities in the north, Gbagbo's frequent references to Ouattara as an "outsider" underlined years of discrimination, while continued economic hardship due first to an economic downturn and eventually international sanctions against the government made many close ranks against non-native Ivorians.

Although fighting stopped almost completely in 2004, it took another three years for a peace agreement to be formally brokered by the United Nations. New elections were to be held as part of the agreement, but it took three years for those elections to take place. Ouattara was elected, and the results were recognized as official by the international community and the African Union, but Gbagbo refused to step down. In 2011, fighting resumed.

During the one-year conflict, violence escalated into a **humanitarian crisis**. Thousands were killed in the fighting, including the massacres of civilians in villages across the country. The international community, which had put in place sanctions against Gbagbo after the election of Ouattara, intervened after concerns about the high number of casualties became an international issue. French and United Nations forces assisted in capturing Gbagbo, his wife, and his son, who were taken to Ouattara's headquarters before being turned over to the UN.

Since the end of the conflict, Ivory Coast has struggled with stability and a lack of **reconciliation**. The economy has remained weak, and a high number of internally displaced persons and refugees have not been able to return to their homes due to fears about their security. Although Ouattara was reelected president in 2015, many of the issues that drove the civil war remain.

Liberian Civil Wars

Liberia also experienced two civil wars back to back, beginning in 1989 and ending in 2003. The first, which took place between 1989 and 1997, killed more than six hundred thousand people and brought Charles Taylor to power. The second, from 1999 to 2003, forced him from power. The conflict was a massive humanitarian crisis, with numerous human rights violations carried out by both sides, including the use of child soldiers.

The foundation was laid for the conflict in 1980, when Samuel Doe took control of the country in a coup. In 1985, Doe held elections for show, and these were not considered free or fair. Four years later, Charles Taylor, a former government official, returned to the country from Ivory Coast and formed the Armed Forces of Liberia, which started an uprising against Doe's rule. Another faction formed around the National Patriotic Front of Liberia, led by former soldier Prince Johnson. Johnson and his forces took control of the capital, Monrovia, in 1990. He also executed Doe, but fighting continued between Johnson's forces and Taylor's forces until 1995, when peace negotiations led by the international community ended the conflict.

In 1997, elections were held and Charles Taylor was elected president. But in

Charles Taylor, former president of Liberia, has been charged with crimes against humanity by international courts.

1999, a rebel group emerged and the second civil war began. The Liberians United for Reconciliation and Democracy (or LURD) was located in the north and backed by neighboring Guinea and later Sierra Leone. In the south, the Movement for Democracy in Liberia joined the fight in 2003, fighting against Taylor in the south and further undermining his hold on power. Taylor countered them with an elite force, called the Anti-Terrorist Unit, and fighters who had been part of the National Patriotic Front of Liberia.

The LURD was made up of various groups opposed to Taylor's rule, and it eventually gained the support of the international community. In 2003, after the Movement for Democracy in Liberia joined the fight, the two groups were able to force Taylor's resignation. At that time, he controlled only around one-third of the country, including the capital of Monrovia. He went into exile in Nigeria before being sent to the international court at The Hague to be tried for war crimes and crimes against humanity.

The Liberian civil wars were both defined by their extreme brutality. More than one million civilians were displaced, and around two hundred and fifty thousand were killed in the fighting. Sexual violence and execution were common during the conflict, as was the use of child soldiers. Many have voiced concern that the government of President Ellen Johnson Sirleaf, the current president and first leader after the civil war, has not done enough to promote reconciliation or to hold those responsible for the crimes accountable.

The Second Liberian Civil War is also an example of a proxy war, or a war in which states fight indirectly. The rebel forces fighting against Taylor's regime were backed by neighboring Guinea and Sierra Leone, both of which provided weapons, training, and financial support. Though the war was a civil conflict, Taylor was effectively fighting against both countries. This is a common war tactic, in part because it helps international states avoid declaring traditional, full war against an enemy and because it lends legitimacy to the forces fighting, hiding any possible influence by a foreign government. But proxy wars are also dangerous, as they can fuel conflict that can bleed over into full war between neighbors and undermine regional security.

Sierra Leone Civil War

The proxy war between Sierra Leone and Liberia also caused prolonged conflict in Sierra Leone, where a civil war started

The years-long civil war in Sierra Leone left much of country's infrastructure, such as schools like this one, in shambles.

with the support of Liberia's Charles Taylor in 1991 lasted until 2002 and killed more than fifty thousand people.

The conflict began when the Revolutionary United Front (RUF) attempted to overthrow the government of Joseph Momoh. The rebel group was supported by the National Patriotic Front of Liberia and Taylor and initially moved quickly against the government. But a **stalemate** of sorts evolved over time, with the government taking back and giving up territory over the next several years. In 1992, a military coup unseated the government of Joseph Momoh, and for a time it appeared RUF was being forced out of the country. In 1996, the RUF and the government signed a peace agreement, but the government withdrew shortly thereafter and the agreement was never implemented.

Fighting continued after the failed agreement, and the next year another coup changed the field. In 1997, the military of Sierra Leone overthrew the government again, and the Armed Revolutionary Council (AFRC) was declared the government of Sierra Leone, and RUF joined it against remaining military forces aligned with a civilian government elected in 1996. AFRC declared the war over when new leader Johnny Paul Koroma captured the capital of Freetown, yet violence continued. The Economic Community of East African States sent in forces to retake Freetown, but the troops were unable to capture the rest of the country.

A United Nations peace agreement was negotiated in 1999. That agreement, called the Lome Peace Accord, nearly fell apart in 2000, when disarmament by RUF proved too slow and rebel groups began advancing on cities. The United Kingdom, Guinea, and the United Nations helped the weak civilian government bring an end to the conflict and begin the process of disarmament. Two years later, the government declared the civil war officially over.

Much like the conflict in Liberia, the Sierra Leone Civil War was marked by human right violations, the use of child soldiers, and extreme brutality. As part of the peace agreement, the Truth and Reconciliation Commission was established to investigate the conflict and provide a means for civilians to openly discuss their trauma. The United Nations also set up a special court, with permission from Sierra Leone, to try those responsible for the atrocities committed during the war. International courts have found leaders in the conflict guilty of war crimes, including terrorism, enslavement, and sexual violence. Charles Taylor was found guilty on similar charges, as well as crimes against humanity, due to his role in the conflict.

Northern Mali Conflict

The Northern Mali Conflict began in early 2012 and has continued since despite a brief peace agreement. The conflict began when the Tuareg, a traditionally nomadic population found in the Sahara region, started fighting the Malian government for an independent state. The National Movement for the Liberation of Azawad (MNLA), a group named for the region of Mali that fighters want established as a new state, received weapons and support from Libyan forces, making them well armed for their struggle against the Malian government. While primarily controlled by the

Tuareg rebel fighters

Tuareg, MNLA also represents other ethnic groups from the Azawad region.

In April 2012, government forces left Azawad following a coup, which took place because of public dissatisfaction with how the government was handling the rebellion in the north. But with government forces gone, differences between the groups fighting against the state escalated into conflict between them. The Islamist Ansar Dine had fought with the MNLA, but in mid-2012 it joined forces with groups like the Movement for Oneness and Jihad in West Africa to fight against MNLA. The group, rather than seeking independence, has a stated goal of forming an Islamic state in Mali. Since 2012, other Islamist groups have become active in the area, including al-Qaeda in the Islamic Maghreb, Ansar al-Sharia, and Boko Haram.

In 2013, French forces entered the conflict to fight against Islamist groups in Azawad. In June of that year, an agreement between the Malian government and the MNLA ended the fighting temporarily. The rebels withdrew from the agreement later that year when they accused Mali of not following through on its commitments to a truce. Another agreement was signed in Algeria in 2015, although attacks are still carried out occasionally and Islamists are still present.

Nigerian Conflict

A war has been raging in north-central Nigeria, although it has received little outside attention since starting in 2001. The conflict is between Christian farmers and Muslim herdsmen, two groups that have long disputed land rights in Nigeria's Middle Belt region. An estimated sixty thousand people have been killed in fighting between the two since 2001, and although the divide rests along religious lines, religion does not appear to play a role in the conflict.

As with many conflicts in Africa, colonial rule played a role in establishing the tensions that eventually led to fighting. The Middle Belt, a traditionally Christian area, was opened up to outside workers by the British colonial administration when it needed people to mine tin. The Fulani, a nomadic tribe of Muslims, began arriving in the area with their livestock. The tribe became settled in the area, but their herds infringed on pasture that had traditionally been farmed by local Christian Berom tribes.

The Berom vocally opposed the presence of the Fulani, but tensions didn't become violent until 2001. Berom farmers and Fulani herdsmen rioted in the city of Jos when regional elections were won by the Christian People's Democratic Party. Supporters of the opposing All Nigeria People's Party had accused officials of rigging the vote, and clashes erupted. In around a week of fighting, more than one thousand people were killed.

It was the spark that set off ongoing violence. Since 2001, Fulani militias have carried out attacks on villages and civilians, which in turn has prompted revenge attacks by the Berom. Although violence is committed by both sides, the Fulani are believed to be carrying out the worst atrocities and responsible for the most deaths. According to witnesses, attacks often take place at night, and people are targeted based on whether those attacking believe they may be part of the rival forces. Brutal tactics, including possible cannibalism, have occurred on both sides of the conflict. Women and children have been the most impacted by the violence. In 2015, the Global Terrorism Index indicated that the Fulani militias were responsible for more than one thousand deaths in the previous year. It also cited possible links between the Fulani and Boko Haram, although the Fulani are only focused on the Middle Belt area.

Despite religious differences, the conflict seems more rooted in land rights and access to resources. Little is known about the Fulani, however, beyond the fact that they have been aggressively targeting farm owners and claiming their land. Overall goals, leadership structure, and potential links to terrorist organizations are largely speculation.

Terrorism in Western Africa

Although terrorism is a security threat in western Africa, it is less widespread than it is in northern Africa. The Maghreb Insurgency impacts several western African states in addition to northern African states, including Mali. While there are several groups with a presence in the region, Boko Haram and al-Qaeda in the Islamic Maghreb have been the most active across state lines. ISIS is believed to have a possibly growing presence in the region, though it is still fighting AQIM for authority.

Boko Haram

Boko Haram emerged in Nigeria in 2002, under the name "People Committed to the Propagation of the Prophet's Teachings and Jihad," shortened to its current name by Nigerians near the group's headquarters. It was first established as a school that rejected Western education, a common practice among Muslims (especially conservative Muslims) since the colonial era. But it soon evolved, and the school became a means to recruit fighters. Boko Haram began targeting the Nigerian government in 2009, with a stated goal of establishing an Islamic state that adheres to the group's extreme vision of Islam. Although the state finally took notice of the group following its early attacks, a massive jail break in 2010 replenished its numbers, and Nigeria has struggled to counter the group's presence ever since.

Boko Haram is one of the most active terrorist groups in Africa and in 2015 allied with the Islamic State.

In 2014, Boko Haram drew international attention and condemnation when it kidnapped two hundred schoolgirls from the village of Chibok, many of whom remain captives. That same year the group pledged allegiance to ISIS, taking on the name Islamic State in West Africa Province, although that name is not often used when referring to the group. The alliance was unexpected, as many had believed Boko Haram was working with al-Qaeda in the Islamic Maghreb, with which ISIS factions in the region have been locked in conflict and rivalry. Today, the group is believed to be broken up into smaller groups. This decentralization, or lack of central authority, is a tactic used by terrorist organizations around the world to make it easier for smaller groups to function individually, so that no one attack against the group can weaken it significantly. Its alliance with ISIS has also signaled

Jihad

In international terrorism, the term "jihad" has become shorthand for the many atrocities Islamist extremist groups carry out against civilians and governments. But the concept is much more complicated than common usage would suggest, and as a tenet of Islam it has many different meanings. In the Quran, the Islamic holy book, jihad refers to the duty of all Muslims to preserve their faith. This gives rise to the commonly applied definition of jihad as "Holy War."

But that one definition is highly controversial. According to Islamic teachings, jihad has two facets. The first, called the "greater jihad," is the struggle within a person to overcome doubts, temptations, and other barriers to connecting with his or her faith. It is a spiritual struggle, rather than a struggle with someone else. Physical jihad, called the "lesser jihad," can be used to describe violent or nonviolent action to defend the faith. It is focused outward toward society, rather than involving reflection on the self. Some consider the spread of the Islamic empire a form of jihad, although the early Caliphates were religiously diverse. Until modern times, "jihadist" violence as we know it was unthinkable, including the targeting of civilians and use of suicide attacks. Those who embrace violent jihad make up a very small minority of Muslims around the world, despite their prominence in the media.

that the group is becoming a regional power, rather than focusing on Nigeria exclusively.

In 2015, a coalition of regional states managed to retake all towns previously under Boko Haram's control, but the group remains an active and dangerous presence in western Africa, carrying out attacks in Niger, Cameroon, and Chad, as well as Nigeria. The group targets civilians as well as military and government sites and has kidnapped many young women and girls to force into marriage with fighters. According to the Council on Foreign Relations, the group has killed more than ten thousand civilians and displaced more than one million.

Al-Qaeda in the Islamic Maghreb

Al-Qaeda in the Islamic Maghreb (AQIM), as discussed in the previous chapter, is very active in the Sahara region, including northern Mali, Burkina Faso, and Benin. The group is an al-Qaeda affiliate, first being formed under the name Salafist Group for Preaching and Combat in Algeria before pledging allegiance to al-Qaeda. AQIM has expressed plans and demonstrated capabilities to carry out attacks on civilians, but the group also targets oil and gas facilities in the region. Additionally, it uses kidnapping of foreign nationals as a means to gain funds, ransoming them to foreign countries and organizations.

As ISIS has expanded its influence in the region, AQIM has also tried to reassert itself as the terrorist organization with the most influence. The threat ISIS posed to AQIM was highlighted in 2015 when regional group Boko Haram changed allegiance to ISIS. In response to ISIS's reach, AQIM has carried out more wide-ranging attacks in recent years, including attacks in Ivory Coast and Senegal. AQIM has explicitly threatened to carry out attacks on civilians, which has made states like Ghana concerned about potentially

Ellen Johnson Sirleaf

Ellen Johnson Sirleaf is the sitting president of Liberia. She was elected in 2005, in the country's first post–civil war elections, and won reelection in 2011. She was the first female president of an African country and came to power in the aftermath of the brutal conflict that tore Liberia apart. Since taking office, she has been working toward reconciliation and economic recovery. She was awarded the Nobel Peace Prize, alongside two other female leaders, in 2011.

One of Sirleaf's first acts as president was the establishment of the Truth and Reconciliation Commission (TRC), which was designed to promote security and unity through a thorough investigation of the civil war. The commission also looked back to 1979 to investigate human rights violations that had taken place in the country, which included war crimes and crimes against humanity. The TRC made recommendations to the government on how to handle those found responsible, including reparations and legal proceedings it felt appropriate. It also provided recommendations on how to avoid similar atrocities in the future. It took three years for the group to release a full report on the conflict, and in it Sirleaf herself was implicated for early support for Charles Taylor. She apologized and has since extradited Taylor so that he can be put on trial for war crimes in Sierra Leone.

being targeted. The group has threatened Morocco, issuing a video showing King Mohammed surrounded by fire. These attacks are intended to show its strength and to counter ISIS propaganda that has called for Sunni Muslims to abandon AQIM and join it instead.

Al-Mourabitoun

One of AQIM's most important allies in western Africa is al-Mourabitoun, which translates to "the Sentinels" in Arabic. The group was formed in 2013, when the Movement for Oneness and Jihad in West Africa merged with the Masked Men Brigade. In 2015 it declared allegiance to AQIM and has since worked closely with the group in the Maghreb. It is based in northern Mali, although it has carried out attacks across western Africa.

The group is multi-ethnic and has members from Mali, Algeria, Tunisia, and the Tuareg. Al-Mourabitoun has carried out attacks in Mali, Burkina Faso, and Ivory Coast, where it took part in a massive attack on a resort that killed tourists and Ivorian civilians. The group has also been involved in taking hostages. Conflicting statements have been released by the group, signaling possible infighting among leadership over whether to be affiliated with ISIS or AQIM, but intelligence at this time shows cooperation with AQIM on multiple attacks.

Rwandan soldiers prepare for an airlift mission in the Central
African Republic, where civil war has continued for years.

3 | Central Africa

entral Africa is a region in the very heart of the continent, with Atlantic coastline to the west and a landlocked border in the east. It includes Burundi, Cameroon, Central African Republic, Chad, Republic of the Congo, the Democratic Republic of the Congo, Equatorial Guinea, Gabon, and São Tomé and Príncipe.

Central Africa has experienced some of the most long-term wars of the twenty-first century, some of which have no end in sight. Political instability has been a driving factor in conflict in the region, making room for rebel groups to take control of large areas. In Central African Republic and the Democratic Republic of the Congo, war has been the norm since the early 2000s and late 1990s, respectively. Chad has been at war consistently since the 1960s, with civil wars taking place during a combined twenty-six years between 1965 and 2010.

While civil conflicts and insurgencies are the most common forms of conflict in the region, the Congo Wars were all-encompassing conflicts between numerous African states. There were two such wars, with the first resulting in the renaming of Zaire as the Democratic Republic of the Congo, where most of the fighting took place. States involved in the conflict, which is discussed in detail below, included Libya in the north and South Africa in the south, as well as numerous states between those two.

The role of terrorism in conflict in central Africa is complicated. Whereas other areas have strong central governments fighting against established terrorist groups, central African states have weak central governments that struggle to confront insurgencies in their territory, control borders, or adequately deal with underlying tensions that fuel fighting. Violence linked to religion is common, with both Christian and Muslim militias active across the region. The region is also home to the notorious Lord's Resistance Army, a rebel group active in both central Africa and Uganda.

Major Wars in Central Africa

Central Africa has experienced long-term and recurring conflicts in the late twentieth and early twenty-first centuries. Civil war is common, but the region has also experienced multicountry conflicts and wars for independence. The frequency of conflict and the prolonged nature of war in the region is due in part to the inability of governments to respond efficiently and political instability, as coups and regime change through war have been common.

Central African Republic Civil Wars

The Central African Republic, or CAR, is in the very center of the region and the African continent. The state has been at war for most of the twenty-first century, experiencing a civil war that ran from 2004 to 2007, resumed in 2012, and continues today.

The first civil war, called the Central African Republic Bush War, began in 2004. In 2003, long-time military and government official Francois Bozize seized power while the sitting, democratically elected president was out of the country, claiming the presidency for himself. In 2004, a coalition of rebel groups, called the Union of Democratic Forces for Unity (UFDR), attempted to overthrow Bozize, sparking the conflict. Several other rebel groups were also involved at various points, including the Democratic Front of the Central African People (FDPC) and the People's Army for the Restoration of Democracy (APRD).

After three years of brutal fighting, the Bush War ended with a cease-fire agreement between FDCP and the government. Another followed in 2008, which was signed by APRD and UFDR. The agreement, called the Global Peace Accord, included provisions for disarmament and amnesty for rebels, as well as integration of fighters into society. But the peace was fragile, and tension still existed on both sides. That tension and distrust lead to the second civil war, which began four years later.

In 2012, rebel groups re-formed and accused the government of not honoring the terms of the peace agreement. In early 2013, a coalition known as Seleka seized the capital and deposed Bozize's government. The group's leader, Michel Djotodia, took over the country and named himself president, becoming the first Muslim leader of the Christian-majority country. Despite being in power, however, Seleka continued carrying out attacks and acts of violence throughout the country, killing civilians and destroying villages. Djotodia tried to disband the militias, but the same group that put him in power proved difficult to control. In early 2014, Djotodia and his prime minister agreed to step down as part of a negotiated attempt at peace. But the change in leadership did not end the fighting.

Early on in the second civil war, religious differences became a focus of fighting. Seleka is made up of Muslim militias, and much of its violence was targeted at the Christian majority, which had ruled the country since independence.

Christian militias were formed in response, known as anti-balaka and started as neighborhood defense forces. But they soon evolved into groups of similar power and brutality, with Christian militias moving into Muslim villages and massacring civilians. Until then, CAR had not experienced **sectarian** violence or conflict, but militias were effectively conducting a religious genocide.

Attempts to end the fighting have proven ineffective, as the weak central government cannot exert control over its territory. As a result, the violence has continued unchecked, despite the presence of foreign troops and a cease-fire signed and abandoned in 2014. Civilians, particularly women and children, have suffered the most. Sexual violence is used by both sides in the conflict, and children struggle with malnutrition and disease, as well as the threat of death or mutilation. More than six thousand people have been killed in the fighting, while more than five hundred thousand have been displaced within the country. Due to fighting, a humanitarian crisis has emerged with more than two million people in need of medical assistance and food.

The Congo Wars

The Congo Wars, two separate conflicts that ran from 1996 to 2003 with around a one-year break between 1997 and 1998, drew in states from across the continent. The Second Congo War is sometimes called the Great War of Africa or the African World War because of the large portion of the continent that became involved. Both wars were fought in the Democratic Republic of the Congo, known as Zaire until the First Congo War. Although the official war ended in 2003, insurgents have continued fighting.

The First Congo War was prompted by several tensions, including the long-term dictatorship of Mobuto Sese Seko

A military parade in Kinshasa marks the fifty-fourth anniversary of the Democratic Republic of the Congo's independence from Belgium

in then-Zaire. Although he had promised reforms under international and domestic pressure, Zaire was a failing state unable to truly provide for or take care of the country. Rebel groups flourished in the farther reaches of the country, particularly the eastern provinces. Ethnic tensions in the migrant-heavy east had led to conflict during the twentieth century, particularly between native tribes and Tutsi migrants from neighboring Rwanda. Following the Rwandan genocide in the 1990s, a large number of both Tutsi and Hutu refugees entered Zaire, including Hutu *genocidaires*, who committed violence in Rwanda.

That mass migration laid the foundation for the First Congo War. The Hutu forces that relocated to Zaire began carrying out attacks against Tutsis in Zaire and the government in Rwanda, and the Zairian government could not control them. As a result, Rwanda mobilized Tutsi militias it had established in eastern Zaire, first with the goal of controlling the east and fighting the Hutu genocidaires. But soon displeasure with the Mobuto government spilled over, and the Tutsi joined forces with the Alliance of Democratic Forces for the Liberation of Congo (AFDL) to fight against the government.

Fighting began in 1996, with the AFDL taking a large territory and targeting Hutu refugees, including civilians. In 1997, with Uganda and Angola sending troops to fight alongside Rwandan and Zairian soldiers, the forces began advancing on the capital to overthrow Mobuto. Zaire's military could not stand up to the rebels, and Mobuto fled to Morocco. Laurent-Desire Kabila, leader of AFDL, took control of the country and announced himself as president. He also changed the name of the country from Zaire to the Democratic Republic of the Congo (DRC).

But despite the change in name and leadership, the situation in the DRC did not get better. The weak economy did not become stronger, and Kabila's government did not give the east more autonomy, although the capital had little control over the area. He centralized power in the capital city of Kinshasa, aggravating tensions with minority ethnic groups. Many also saw him as a representative of the foreign governments that helped put him in power, pushing Kabila to turn his back on Rwanda, Uganda, and Angola and forcing their troops out of the country. In 1998, Rwanda was faced with an insurgency by Hutu forces based in eastern DRC, and its lack of troops in the DRC made it difficult for it to combat the threat. Soon after, the army turned on the central government and began working with the Rwandan and Ugandan governments against Kabila's leadership. This sparked the Second Congo War.

Unlike during the First Congo War, when the rebels faced little resistance as they marched on the capital and overthrew the government, the Kabila government had powerful allies. The rebels, including the Rally for Congolese Democracy (RCD) and factions of the Congolese military, were assisted by Rwanda, Uganda, and Burundi. But the DRC was aided directly by Angola, Namibia, and Zimbabwe; supported indirectly by Sudan, Chad, and CAR; helped logistically by Libya; and supported politically by South Africa, Zambia, and Tanzania.

Despite the strong turnout for Kabila, the outcome was far from clear. Forces on both sides advanced and retreated, and the war turned into a multi-front effort as troops entered the country from neighboring states. The assassination of Kabila in 2001 was a turning point. His son Joseph Kabila was sworn into office and proved a better political leader. He met with the president of Rwanda and was able to put in place a United Nations–drafted plan to end the war. When the tide began turning against Rwanda and rebel forces in 2002, many fighters abandoned the fight. A peace agreement was negotiated that year, and the conflict was ended formally in 2003. The agreement allowed Joseph Kabila to maintain power in a multiparty government and provided for the disarmament of DRC-based Hutu militias.

The war had ended, but the ongoing fighting and lack of central government took a much longer toll on the population. In 2008, more than five million had died due to the conflict and its effects, including malnutrition and disease. Many of those deaths were from preventable diseases, which could have been nonfatal if medical assistance was available. The conflict is the deadliest in African history and the deadliest in the world since World War II. Millions were displaced internally and forced to flee the country.

International forces, including United Nations missions, have played a role in bringing stability to war-torn countries.

Ituri Conflict

While most conflicts in the region focus on government forces versus rebel groups, the Ituri Conflict of 1999 to 2003 pitted two rival ethnic groups against each other in a violent, deadly war. The two groups are located in the Ituri region, which is in northeastern Democratic Republic of the Congo. It was preceded by a low-level conflict, which started in 1972 and began again shortly after the war officially ended.

The conflict was between the Lendu and the Hema ethnic groups. The two groups had been long-time rivals due to favoritism shown to the Hema by the Belgian colonial leaders when the country was part of the Belgian imperial colonies. The Belgian authorities so favored the Hema that they became more educated and wealthier than the Lendu, which in turn caused conflict. This practice was common for the Belgian forces. It was in part what fed the rivalry between the Hutu and Tutsi in Rwanda, leading to the Rwandan Genocide discussed in the next chapter. By dividing ethnic groups and playing them off of each other, colonial powers were able to cut off any possible coalition against their rule.

When the DRC became independent, the Lendu and Hema were left with land disagreements that soon turn to conflict. These disagreements were exacerbated in 1973, when a land-use law made it legal for people to buy land they did not live on and force residents to leave, which undermined families who had lived on land for generations and were not aware it was being bought or sold. In 1972, 1985, and 1996 these arguments brought about fighting.

The conflict began following the Second Congo War, when weapons and fighters flooded into the region. When a Ugandan-backed rebel leader declared the Ituri region in 1999, he also named a Hema the governor. The Lendu feared that the Ugandan government was backing the Hema, and fighting broke out between the two groups' militias. It continued until 2003, when peacekeeping forces moved into the area in hopes of ending the violence. But while they managed to largely stabilize and disarm the region, the fighting continues on and off today between militiamen resistant to reconciliation.

Refugee camps in Chad house displaced people forced to flee ongoing fighting and civil conflict.

Chad Civil War

Chad has been plagued by conflict since gaining independence in 1960. The country is divided between the Muslim north and Christian south, a division underlined by ethnic tension between the two regions; Chad is the northernmost central African state and has both ethnically Arab and ethnically sub-Saharan populations. The country has been at near-constant war since 1965, with power passing back and forth between the northerners and southerners. Most conflict erupts in response to one group being in power; the other side will launch a war to take power back. Although there was a sixteen-year period of calm between 1982 and 1998, a civil war started in 1998 lasted until 2002.

The latest civil war in Chad began in late 2005 and lasted until early 2010. The country had been struggling with a large number of refugees from the conflict in neighboring Darfur and DRC. At the same time, Janjaweed fighters had begun crossing the border from Sudan to attack Chadian villages and civilians. Fighting began after President Idriss Deby amended the constitution to let himself run for third term. In response, the already weakened army saw massive desertions, undermining Deby's authority. Rebel groups began forming coalitions soon after, including the Rally for Democracy and Liberation (RDL), the Platform for Unity, Democracy and Change (SCUD), and United Front for Democracy and Change (FUCD). Their stated aim was to overthrow the Deby government.

The civil war took place against a backdrop of hostility between Sudan and Chad, and that simmering conflict shaded the war. Chad alleged that Sudan was supporting rebels in an attempt to achieve regime change, while Sudan accused the Chadian government of backing rebels in Darfur.

The conflict came to an end in 2010, when Sudan and Chad signed a peace agreement. The agreement opened the border between the two countries and provided a framework for cooperation on border security. The United Nations also set up a working group to help provide security for the humanitarian groups in the country, training policy, and ensuring security for refugee camps.

Uganda has been able to largely push out the LRA, one of the continent's most deadly and long-lasting terrorist organizations.

Terrorism in Central Africa

Central Africa is uniquely placed near the intersection of several terrorist organizations' sphere of influence. Chad, the northernmost country in the region, is just beyond the influence of al-Qaeda in the Islamic Maghreb and terrorist groups in Libya, but Boko Haram has carried out attacks in the country. To the east, al-Shabaab is active along the coast but has not spread inland. Central African states more often struggle with internal groups and regional organizations like the notorious Lord's Resistance Army (LRA). Unguarded borders make it easy for groups like LRA to cross between countries.

Katanga Insurgency

The Katanga Insurgency in the DRC has been ongoing in one form or another since 1960. Katanga is a province in southeastern DRC, but it was divided into four separate provinces under the 2015 constitution. Despite this, the rebels in the area, including the Mai Mai Kata Katanga, have been fighting for an independent state in the area.

The conflict began soon after the DRC (then called Zaire) became independent in 1960. A tribal federation declared the State of Katanga, but attempts to defend the area failed and it became part of the DRC in 1963. Two major insurgencies took place in the late 1970s, called Shaba I and Shaba II, but the fighting remained low-level for the rest of the twentieth century. The fight was revived in 2011, when Gedeon Kyungu Mutanga was able to escape from prison. He established the Mai Mai Kata Katanga and the Mai Mai Gedeon, the two latest rebel groups to take up the banner of Katangan independence. To date, the conflict has forced hundreds of thousands to flee the area and killed an unknown number of people, although the toll is estimated in the thousands. The use of child soldiers by the militias is common, and the United Nations is involved in providing humanitarian aid. Although Mutanga turned himself in to international authorities in 2006, commanders remain in the field and the fighting continues today.

Allied Democracy Forces

The Allied Democracy Forces (ADF) has been active for more than twenty years. The group was started in Uganda in 1989 when the Muslim Tablighi Jamaat merged with the National Army for the Liberation of Uganda. They carried out their first attack in Uganda in 1996, targeting villages along the Uganda-DRC border. In the late 1990s they attacked cities, kidnapped students, and released prisoners from jail. But Uganda began a harsh crackdown on the group in 2007, forcing the remaining rebels into the DRC, where they are now active.

Centered in the mountains between the North Kivu region of the DRC and Uganda, the group was believed to have around 1,500 members as of 2015. Despite setbacks due to a joint United Nations-DRC effort to combat them, the group has remained present in the country. When the group was founded, its stated goal was to overthrow the Ugandan government and replace it with a fundamentalist Islamic state, but it is unclear if the group still hopes to do this. Since being forced out of Uganda, ADF has been focused on attacks in North Kivu and villages, killing scores of people and forcing others to flee.

ADF was founded by a Muslim and once called for the formation of an Islamic state, but the group isn't believed to be Islamist or Jihadist. It has been suspected of working with extremist groups like al-Shabaab, Boko Haram, and the LRA, as well as the Sudanese government. The tactics witnesses have reported seeing used by the group are similar to ISIS in their brutality, including forced marriage of women hostages and the use of public execution. But its local focus makes it difficult for experts to weigh in on what its motives may be, beyond controlling a small area of the DRC.

Burundi Civil War

As discussed in this chapter and the next chapter, ethnic tension has been a driving force behind some of the worst conflicts in central and eastern Africa in the past three decades. In Rwanda, the 1994 genocide against the Tutsi minority killed hundreds of thousands and became an international humanitarian crisis. Less known is the Burundi Civil War, a conflict that has roots in similar tensions between the Tutsi and Hutu ethnic groups. Under colonial rule, the long-peaceful Tutsi and Hutu ethnic groups were pitted against each other by enforcing ethnic divisions that had long been forgotten. The colonial powers also favored the Tutsis, granting them rights to education and positions of power.

The Burundi Civil War, which lasted from 1994 to 2005, was preceded by two genocides carried out by the Tutsi-controlled army against the Hutu minority. The first genocide took place in 1972 and killed an unknown number of people. The second genocide, in 1993, took place after the assassination of the country's Hutu president, and an estimated twenty-five thousand Tutsi were killed. The civil war started the next year, when another presidential assassination fueled tensions. In 1996, a coup replaced a power-sharing government arrangement between the Hutu and Tutsi with Tutsi control. Hutu rebels responded by targeting Tutsis, and fighting continued until 2005, when almost all rebel groups in the country agreed to a cease-fire.

Lord's Resistance Army

The Lord's Resistance Army (LRA) is another group that started in Uganda but has since spread to CAR and the DRC, as well as South Sudan. It was started in 1986 and is one of the oldest rebel groups in the region. It is considered a terrorist organization by the United States, and executive orders by the president have placed sanctions on the group's leader, Joseph Kony. The group is known for the use of child soldiers, extreme violence against civilians, and the use of sexual violence.

The LRA was founded in 1986, when Joseph Kony took control of a cult-like group calling for the overthrow of the Ugandan government. The group came together in the aftermath of the Ugandan Bush War, which saw violence take place along ethnic lines in the diverse northern Uganda. To fight back, rebel groups were formed, including the LRA. Kony advocated for a government based on the Ten Commandments of Christianity, reflecting the group's origins as a Christian militia. But he also put himself at the center of the cult, using fear and intimidation to control his followers.

The question of what the LRA hopes to achieve has long plagued experts, in part because the group is so tightly controlled by Kony. Initially, the LRA promoted itself as a pro-Acholi militia fighting for the Acholi ethnic minority in northern Uganda. Yet as Ugandan forces have closed in on the group, it has moved to neighboring countries to carry out more violence.

The LRA is known for being extremely violent, and the use of child soldiers is one of the group's most famous practices. In 2012, the group was estimated to have only around three hundred members, but their ranks have been growing through kidnapping. Children are used in violent attacks, drugged or brainwashed so that they do not resist, and then manipulated into staying due to the actions they carry out. Adults are also abducted, although less often and not for combat. Girls are forced into marriage with fighters. According to Human Rights Watch, between 1987 and 2006 the group kidnapped at least twenty thousand Ugandan children and displaced almost two million people. Civilians are also threatened with extreme violence, including mutilation, sexual violence, and torture.

Somali refugees, like those shown here, have been forced
from their country by ongoing war, poverty, and terrorism.

4 | Eastern Africa

astern Africa, which includes the Horn of Africa, rests along the Indian Ocean. It includes Comoros, Djibouti, Eritrea, Ethiopia, Kenya, Madagascar, Mauritius, Rwanda, Seychelles, Somalia, South Sudan, Sudan, Uganda, and Tanzania. Many of these countries have been involved in conflicts with states in central Africa, such as Rwanda, Sudan, and Uganda. Those conflicts are discussed in the previous chapter.

War, terrorism, and politics are closely linked in eastern Africa, where several states have seen unrest in the late twentieth and early twenty-first centuries. Some states, such as Kenya and Rwanda, have emerged from conflict with relative stability. Others, including Sudan and Somalia, have struggled to overcome tensions and years of fighting. South Sudan, the world's youngest country, fell into civil war shortly after declaring independence and is considered a fragile or failed state. The region also saw numerous cross-border conflicts during the twentieth century, pitting neighboring states against one another and shading relations today.

Many of the issues that have caused conflict in eastern Africa can be traced back to the colonial era. Colonial powers, including Belgium and Great Britain, used divisions between ethnic groups to maintain their hold on power by undercutting possible coalitions between tribes. Those divisions eventually resulted in conflict, such as the Rwandan Genocide. Colonial policies also undermined local economies and disrupted traditional farming practices, situations that became deadly when famine struck and food insecurity resulted in starvation and widespread malnutrition during times of war.

Eastern Africa has also seen several secessionist movements, including in Eritrea, Somalia, and Sudan. The groundwork for these conflicts was laid by colonial policies, which favored some groups over others and allowed power to become consolidated in select hands. Colonial policy also drew borders around areas that did not necessarily belong in one state, leading to tension between ruling governments and regions that felt they deserved autonomy. Eritrea became independent from Ethiopia in 1991, and South Sudan successfully broke away from Sudan in 2011, while areas like Somaliland in Somalia continue to agitate for independence.

Major Wars in Eastern Africa

Eastern Africa has seen numerous conflicts in the past three decades. Those discussed below are some of the most significant, highlighting ethnic tension, post-conflict resolution, and civil war. These conflicts also explore the complex legacy of colonial power dynamics that states continue to struggle with post-independence.

Darfur Conflict

The Darfur Conflict, which began in 2003 and continues today, is one of the largest humanitarian crises in modern history. The ongoing fighting began in Sudan's Darfur region between groups advocating for the area's non-Arab

Omar al-Bashir

population and the government, which they accused of oppression. The conflict has killed scores of people and forced an estimated three million to flee into neighboring states, including Chad. The president of Sudan, Omar al-Bashir, has also been indicted by the International Criminal Court for war crimes, genocide, and crimes against humanity as a result of the conflict.

Fighting began in early 2003, but tensions between the Darfur province and the larger Sudanese state can be traced back much earlier. The area was independent for much of history, only becoming a province of Sudan after World War I. The population that lives in Darfur is largely non-Arab, while the government based in Khartoum is Islamist and identifies as Arab. This ethnic difference has underlined tensions caused by a lack of access to water and disputes between nomadic peoples and agriculturalists. In the early 1990s, the Sudanese government was accused of oppressing the non-Arab population with policies that segregated them from the larger, Arab population of the state. The state's policies have been called apartheid.

The Darfur Conflict started when Darfur-based rebel groups the Sudan Liberation Army (SLA) and the Justice and Equality Movement (JEM) carried out a wave of attacks on government targets. When fighting started, SLA and JEM were able to claim territory from the government, but the tide soon turned. In response to the continued attacks, Sudan began carrying out airstrikes in Darfur and used the Janjaweed (Arab militias the government has used in the past to stem uprisings) to carry out what the international community has called genocide.

Although many cease-fire agreements have been signed and peace talks have been held, the violence has shown no signs of stopping. The Sudanese government has continued to use extreme violence against the people of Darfur, with some being forced to flee multiple times due to ongoing fighting. The Janjaweed have largely targeted civilians, and reports claim that they patrol near refugee camps (where international security forces ensure safety) and kill anyone who leaves the immediate area. The rebel forces fighting for Darfur have splintered, giving rise to numerous groups and coalitions, some of which are excluded from negotiations.

As of early 2016, the fighting and targeting of civilians continued. Government forces have pushed into Jebel Marra, in western Darfur, and violence reportedly displaced thirty-four thousand people in just ten days. Malnutrition continues to be a significant issue among refugees and those still living in Darfur, and the near complete destruction of the region has left the agricultural economy in ruins. Despite the presence of United Nations peacekeepers, the fighting shows no signs of stopping. It has also destabilized neighboring countries, including CAR and Chad, as huge influxes of refugees strain already struggling governments and the Janjaweed cross borders to target those from Darfur.

South Sudan Civil War

South Sudan is the world's youngest country, formally becoming independent from Sudan in 2011. Although granted independence through a referendum, South Sudan fought two wars against the Sudanese government before Khartoum agreed to allow the region to hold that referendum. Since then, South Sudan has descended into civil war and is considered a failed state.

The foundation for conflict between the north and south was set when Sudan was still under British control. The colonial administration favored the north, giving power to northern leaders and placing the capital in the northern city of Khartoum. The south is also predominantly sub-Saharan rather than Arab, giving rise to similar ethnic tensions as seen in Darfur. Despite committing to giving the south autonomy after independence in 1956, the northern government did not follow through.

The first Sudanese Civil War between the north and south began in 1955 and lasted until 1972. It was prompted by the arrest and trial of a southern leader but quickly morphed into a call for an independent state. The war ended with an agreement that did not address the many tensions and distrust between the north and south, and the second Sudanese Civil War began in 1983. That conflict lasted until 2005, resulting in an agreement to hold a referendum on independence in South Sudan, which was ultimately held in 2011.

The South Sudanese Civil War began in 2013, just two years after independence was declared. The conflict started when President Salva Kiir began consolidating power and dismissing many top-ranking officials. Among those dismissed was Vice President Riek Machar, who spoke out against Kiir and announced his intention to run in the next presidential election slated to be held in 2015. Although it is unclear who initiated the fighting—both Kiir and Machar claimed the other's followers attacked first—in December 2013, fighting broke out across the country between supporters of the two men. The conflict has since spread beyond the two men's supporters, with militias targeting civilians.

As of 2016, the conflict had killed thousands and displaced an estimated two million people. Cease-fire agreements have yet to hold, with both sides continuing violence while blaming their opponents. In April 2016, Machar was officially sworn in as vice president once again, as per an agreement signed in 2015. But violence continues unabated, with civilians being targeted. Ethnic violence has increased, with ethnic Dinka militias targeting ethnic Fartit populations as recently as July 2016. The ongoing fighting has disrupted the agricultural economy severely, leading to food shortages and threatening up to four million people with malnutrition and starvation.

Rwandan Genocide

Although the Rwandan Genocide took place in 1994, it stands as one of the largest humanitarian crises in African history and one of the most brutal examples of **ethnic cleansing** in modern history. The conflict took place over just one hundred days, between the ethnic groups the Hutu and the Tutsi. It was led by the Hutu-controlled government against the Tutsi minority and killed up to one million Rwandans.

The Rwandan Genocide was a brief but deadly ethnic conflict that left hundreds of thousands dead.

The Tutsi and the Hutu lived in peace for centuries, becoming so fully integrated that any ethnic differences were largely erased. But when Belgium colonized the area, it put in place a system that favored the Tutsi, whom it perceived as superior to the Hutu. The Tutsi were given access to education, positions of power, and other advantages that the Hutu were not given, creating tension between the two groups. The Belgian colonial administration also forced people to carry identification cards noting their ethnic group. This undercut similarities further, formalizing the differences between the two groups.

Tensions continued to simmer after independence in 1962, with clashes between the Hutu and Tutsi taking place frequently. In 1990, rebel group the Rwandan Patriotic Front (RPF) invaded Rwanda from Uganda, kicking off a four-year civil war that pitted the Hutu and Tutsi against one another. In April 1994, president and Hutu moderate Juvenal Habyarimana was assassinated. Hutu extremists were eventually found responsible by international investigations, but at the time the Hutu leadership told supporters that Tutsi fighters were responsible for the killing. In response, they put into motion a plan for ethnic genocide against the Tutsi.

The genocide began shortly after Habyarimana's death and had been planned by the political elite. The RPF was present in the country but unable to counter the wave of violence sweeping the nation. The United Nations also had a presence in Rwanda but was strictly ordered not to become involved in fighting. Civilians as well as militias were involved in the killing, which is believed to have resulted in the deaths of between eight hundred thousand and one million Tutsi, as well as a smaller number of Hutu. The genocide ended in part because communities killed every Tutsi among them, nearly wiping out the Tutsi population of the country. It came to an end officially in July 1994, when the RPF was able to take the capital and control of the country.

Since the end of the conflict, Rwanda has worked hard to overcome the ethnic divisions that led to the genocide and grapple with the legacy of violence and trauma it left in its wake. The country has banned identification along ethnic lines and has put in place councils to help communities reconcile. Rwanda also set up the Gacaca Courts, which, alongside the International Criminal Tribunal of Rwanda, were charged with identifying what happened leading up to and during the genocide, who was responsible for it, and ensuring those responsible are held to justice.

Somali Civil War

Since 1991, Somalia has been embroiled in ongoing conflict. The lack of central government and ongoing instability has allowed for the growth of terrorist group al-Shabaab, discussed in greater detail in the following section. The fighting began with a civil war, which created a power vacuum that further fed the conflict.

In 1991, fighting between rebel groups and the government escalated as the capital of Mogadishu fell to the United Somali Congress (USC) and toppled the government of authoritarian president Mohammed Said Barre. USC was just one of many groups fighting in the country, none of which agreed to work with USC once it had taken control of the country. Within USC, commanders Mohamed Farah Aidid and Ali Mahdi Mohamed clashed as they both sought power, with Mohamed Farah Aidid eventually declaring himself president. But fighting continued between warring factions and militias, and the country had no effective central government for almost twenty years. Instead it was controlled by warlords, with northern Puntland and Somaliland effectively becoming independent.

Although attempts were made by UN and US forces to establish stability throughout the 1990s, it wasn't until 2012 that a central government was put in place. In recent years, the government has worked to reform the state and begin the recovery process, but the presence of al-Shabaab, which once controlled the capital and is still active in the region, has consistently posed a challenge to stability. The group uses Somali territory as a base of operations, from which it attacks Kenya and other neighboring states.

The ongoing fighting in the country posed numerous humanitarian concerns, but these concerns were also exacerbated by famine, flooding, drought, and other factors, such as piracy, which endangered shipments arriving by sea. The lack of a central government and economy gave rise to a vibrant black market and made it nearly possible to ensure humanitarian aid was received by those most in need.

Kenyan Crisis

The Kenyan Crisis in 2007 and 2008 highlights the close relationship between politics and conflict. The internal conflict began in late 2007, when incumbent president Mwai Kibaki was named the winner of that year's presidential elections. His opponent, Raila Odinga, claimed the results were fraudulent, based in part on polls that had shown him ahead of Kibaki for months before the election. When Kibaki was inaugurated just a few days later, the country erupted into violence.

Although protests started out peacefully and with Odinga's support, they soon escalated into violence. The police responded with force, which was shown on television and further stoked the unrest. Violence along ethnic lines soon followed, with many targeting the Kikuyu people, the tribe to which Kibaki belongs. Across the country people clashed with government forces, while Odinga and his Orange Democratic Movement continued to call for protests against Kibaki's presidency.

The fighting lasted until February 2008, when a power-sharing arrangement was agreed to by both Kibaki and Odinga. Under the arrangement, Kibaki remained president while Odinga became prime minister. In that short amount of time the crisis lasted, around fifteen hundred people were killed and up to six hundred thousand were displaced. Although the conflict ended and the country was stabilized, it highlighted the deep ethnic tensions that still exist in

Though largely stable since independence, Kenya has seen riots and ethnic violence in recent years.

Kenyan culture. It remains unclear how much of a role Odinga and other political figures had in the ethnically targeted violence, but witnesses claim that authorities did nothing to stop it. Violence against men and women was extreme, with churches burnt while people took refuge inside and machete attacks taking place around the country. In 2016, protests for electoral reforms turned deadly when riot police responded with force, signaling that although the crisis ended in 2008, the same tensions could lead to violence once again.

Eritrean-Ethiopian War

Eritrea and Ethiopia have a long-running and complex history. Eritrea was part of Ethiopia until 1991, when the

Al-Shabaab has carried out attacks in Somalia and Kenya and is allied with al-Qaeda.

region was allowed to hold a referendum on independence and Eritrea became its own state. Prior to that, Eritreans fought a thirty-year war for independence, which coincided with the Ethiopian Civil War of 1974–1991. When the civil war concluded and the referendum was held in 1991, Eritrea and Ethiopia were controlled by transitional governments headed by former allies. The Tigrayan People's Liberation Front (TPLF) had fought with the Eritrean People's Liberation Front (EPLF) against the government of Derg. Derg was a group that took control of Ethiopia in the coup that launched the civil war in 1974. Now the former allies were across the negotiation table from one another, working to establish the borders between their countries and pave the way for a smooth transition to independence.

But the two groups struggled to agree, and eventually a commission set up to help them negotiate was dissolved. Borders were an issue, and neither side was willing to give up what they felt to be rightfully theirs. The disagreement lingered until 1997, when another commission was set up to try and resolve the issue, but attempts to do so only resulted in more disagreement between the two countries. This led to fights along the border, started by the deaths of several Eritrean officials near the town of Badme. Eritrea responded by sending troops into the area, which was considered part of Ethiopia.

The conflict quickly escalated into total war between the two states, with fighting on three fronts along the border. At times the fighting entered Somalia, as both Eritrea and Ethiopia tried to gain the advantage. The fighting continued until 2000, when a peace agreement was reached between the two states that established a secure zone under United Nations jurisdiction. By then, an estimated seventy thousand had been killed in the fighting.

While the conflict was formally ended, tensions still exist along the border, and skirmishes between Eritrean and Ethiopian forces have taken place as recently as 2012, when Ethiopian troops attacked an Eritrean base on claims that it was hiding rebels.

Terrorism in Eastern Africa

Terrorism and conflict are closely linked in eastern Africa, where al-Shabaab has become one of the most significant security threats to states like Somalia, Kenya, and Ethiopia. The region is also seeing the growth of ISIS, which is competing with al-Qaeda (al-Shabaab's ally) for influence.

Kenyan Mau Mau

The legacy of colonialism has greatly impacted eastern Africa, shaping today's conflicts and creating tension between groups. In Kenya, that legacy includes the Mau Mau, a group of fighters who led a resistance against the British colonial forces from 1952 to 1960. At the time, the British responded with extreme force, mass arrests, sexual violence, and torture. Today, those arrested as part of the crackdown on the Mau Mau continue to call for justice and compensation from the British government.

The Mau Mau was formed in the early 1950s due to unrest over marginalization of the Kikuyu by white settlers. It was established by more radical activists within the existing Kenya African Union, a political group that was calling for greater political rights and land reforms. In 1952, the Mau Mau began carrying out raids and attacks on white-owned farms, prompting the British to declare a state of emergency. Under the state of emergency, the British forced thousands from their homes, arrested more than one hundred fifty thousand people, and killed or tortured an estimated ninety thousand. British soldiers beat those who were arrested, tortured them, and used sexual violence as a punishment. Victims, many of whom are still alive today, have filed lawsuits with the British government for the crimes committed against them by colonial forces, but the British government has fought against each suit despite acknowledging the mistreatment of Kenyans. The Mau Mau Uprising is considered one of the most significant steps against colonial rule in Kenya.

Al-Shabaab

Al-Shabaab emerged in Somalia during the country's ongoing civil war. It was a military wing of the Islamic Courts Union, which controlled the capital city of Mogadishu in 2006. The ICU was forced from power by Ethiopian and Somali troops that same year, and al-Shabaab, a name that translates to "the Youth," moved into the south, where it still operates today.

Despite near-constant infighting among its leaders, al-Shabaab has maintained a presence in eastern Africa for more than a decade. The group is aligned with al-Qaeda, although it operates independently from the **core Al-Qaeda** group in the Middle East. Experts are unclear on what al-Shabaab wants in terms of goals, due in part to the loss of most of its highest-ranking leaders in recent years. Some believe the group is divided between those who want to focus on retaking control of Somalia and those who want to carry out cross-border attacks with the support of Gulf-based extremists.

Al-Shabaab has carried out regular attacks in Kenya, Djibouti, and Somalia, and has allegedly planned attacks against Ethiopia. In the territory it controls, the group enforces an interpretation of sharia law, with strict bans on lawful activities. Music, movies, smoking, and the shaving of beards are illegal, with punishments including amputations and stoning. Reports have also suggested that the group is using child soldiers, a practice common among rebel groups in central Africa and eastern Africa.

Al-Shabaab is not the only Islamist group in the region, and it has merged with others in recent years. This includes Al Hijra, a Kenyan group originally called the Muslim Youth Center; Ansar Muslim Youth Center, a Tanzanian group; and the Allied Democratic Forces in the Democratic Republic of the Congo.

The Janjaweed

The Janjaweed are Arab militias that have been prominent in
the ongoing conflict in Darfur, Sudan. The militias are believed
to have roots in Libya's Islamic League and Arab Gathering, two
groups that emphasized the Arab ethnicity of parts of eastern
and central Africa's populations. The group was active in Darfur
for at least a decade before the conflict began, although its
raids were focused primarily on taking cattle from non-Arab
farmers. That changed in 2003, when the onset of fighting in
Darfur mobilized the Janjaweed as an unofficial branch of the
Sudanese military.

The Janjaweed, usually on horses or camels, enter villages
and massacre non-Arab civilians. Their attacks are often
preceded by aerial strikes by the Sudanese government,
which suggests close cooperation between the two groups.
The Janjaweed are led primarily by a man named Musa Hilal,
who is said to be the most brutal of the group's leadership.
He was a tribal leader before becoming a central organizer
of the Janjaweed, and today he is at the center of the ethnic
cleansing of the region. The militias are known for looting
and destroying the homes of those they attack, as well as
patrolling near refugee camps to target anyone who wanders
too far away from safety and for carrying out attacks against
refugees as they flee. The Sudanese government denies
using the Janjaweed in Darfur, but international observers say
investigations show clear cooperation.

Jahba East Africa

Al-Qaeda has had a presence in eastern Africa, particularly the Horn of Africa, for decades. But ISIS, al-Qaeda's primary rival in the Middle East and Africa, has also begun establishing itself in the region. Jahba East Africa, a new group made up of former members of al-Shabaab, pledged allegiance to ISIS in 2016. Experts believe ISIS had been courting al-Shabaab leadership for some time before the group split along ISIS versus al-Qaeda lines following Boko Haram's decision to switch allegiance in 2015.

Although Jahba East Africa is still new, its existence points to a growing tension between al-Qaeda and ISIS across Africa. Al-Qaeda has had an established presence on the continent for decades. On the other hand, ISIS has slowly encroached through strategic alliances and the establishment of loyal branches in each of al-Qaeda's spheres of influence. Despite the fact that this could lead to attacks on one another, this rivalry does not mean that either group is less likely to target civilians. As we've seen in western Africa, where al-Qaeda has increased attacks in an attempt to prove its superiority, competition between terrorist organizations can result in more violence against the general population. It could also exacerbate existing issues, including malnutrition and economic instability, which will make reconstruction and governance all the more difficult for fragile states.

Nelson Mandela, once considered a terrorist, was an advocate for peace in South Africa and across the continent.

5 Southern Africa

Southern Africa rests at the very southern tip of the continent, bordered by both the Atlantic Ocean and the Indian Ocean. It includes Angola, Botswana, Lesotho, Malawi, Mozambique, Namibia, South Africa, Swaziland, Zambia, and Zimbabwe.

Southern Africa has experienced conflict and war in the past, but the region is largely stable today. The two largest wars in the area came to an end in the late 1990s and early 2000s, although at their height many regional states were involved in the fighting. Zimbabwe, despite being a dictatorship that regularly experiences violence committed by the state, has not experienced widespread unrest, and other states have not become involved in cross-border conflicts or civil wars during the twenty-first century. South Africa, the most powerful country in the region, also found a political solution to end apartheid, avoiding a possible civil war between the African majority and the ruling white minority.

Terrorism has also not been a significant threat in the region, although Zimbabwe experiences state terrorism regularly. No international terrorist organizations have a presence in the region, and despite occasional terror alerts, no large-scale terrorist attacks have been carried out since 2000. This does not mean that southern Africa is immune to terrorism; in fact, the region has seen how groups can be radicalized, as discussed below. But southern Africa has resources that some states in Africa don't, including strong central governments and controlled borders, which makes it more difficult for groups like al-Qaeda and ISIS to establish a foothold in the region.

Major Wars in Southern Africa

Southern Africa has been largely stable since 2000, with a few long-term conflicts ending in the first few years of the twenty-first century. Since then no large conflicts have broken out in the region. In Namibia, once part of South Africa, the transition to independence in the 1990s took place peacefully and without conflict.

During the two major conflicts in the region, proxy wars developed. In Angola and Mozambique, both of which experienced long civil wars after gaining independence, neighboring states became involved early on to try to influence the outcome. The United States and the Soviet Union also used these conflicts as proxy wars during the Cold War. Conflicts in both countries have left a legacy of displacement, tension, and violence that has continued to cause problems for those in power, and in Mozambique rebel groups continue to clash with security forces.

Mozambican Civil War

The Mozambican Civil War was one of the most brutal and deadly in the history of modern southern African.

Although fighting has ended in Mozambique, unmarked land mines continue to threaten civilians.

The Angolan Civil War raged for years, resulting in the destruction of vital infrastructure and the loss of numerous lives.

The conflict began in 1977, just two years after independence, and lasted until 1992. The war was fought primarily between the ruling Front for Liberation of Mozambique (FRELIMO) and the Mozambique Resistance Movement (RENAMO).

FRELIMO was one of the primary groups fighting against Portuguese control of Mozambique and upon independence declared the country a one-party Socialist state. The ruling party also forced white Mozambicans to leave the country and restructured the political and cultural makeup of the country so severely that the economy collapsed. Neighboring countries, still controlled by a white minority, saw Mozambique—and the also newly independent Angola—as threats to their power. So in response to Mozambique's new government, white-controlled Rhodesia sponsored the rebel group RENAMO against FRELIMO's rule. The Rhodesian army freed an ex-FRELIMO leader from a Mozambican re-education camp in 1977, training him and installing him as the head of RENAMO, although he died during the group's first attack.

After the death of its first leader, RENAMO developed into a **guerrilla** army, targeting infrastructure and hiding in remote areas. Civilians were also forced to work with RENAMO, either as child soldiers or producing and finding supplies. FRELIMO countered its attacks by heavily guarding primary roads and power lines that crossed the country. Both sides relied heavily on the use of land mines, which continued to maim and kill civilians for years after the war.

The conflict evolved into a proxy war between the West and the Soviet Union on the side of FRELIMO and Kenya, Rhodesia, and South Africa on the side of RENAMO. Other regional states eventually got involved, including

Malawi, which supported both sides, and Zimbabwe, which had military bases in Mozambique and backed FRELIMO. By 1978, South Africa was the only country supporting RENAMO. The South African government signed a nonaggression agreement with FRELIMO that year. Under the agreement, South Africa pledged not to attack Mozambique as long as FRELIMO did not support the African National Congress in a revolt against the white-controlled government in South Africa. Support for RENAMO dropped significantly after that agreement was signed but did not end completely until 1990, when the apartheid government in South Africa fell.

After years of stalemate, the war came to an official end when a peace agreement was signed by the president of Mozambique and the leader of RENAMO. From 1992 to 1994, the United Nations provided peacekeepers to oversee the country's transition to democracy. By the time the conflict ended, an estimated one million people had died as a result of the war and famine, with another five million displaced, or about 20 percent of the country's population.

RENAMO, however, was not fully ready to give up the fight and in 2016 began carrying out attacks in the Gorongosa region of the country. Although RENAMO became an official political party after the civil war, its leader, Afonso Dhlakama, has been in hiding since 2014 after alleging that the elections that year were rigged. He has since declared that he plans to take control of more than half of Mozambique's provinces. Since then, security forces and RENAMO fighters have clashed, and human rights violations are believed to be taking place. Mass graves have been found in the area, and witnesses have reported looting, executions, and sexual violence against civilians.

Angolan Civil War

Angola was at war for almost the entire second half of the twentieth century. The country first fought a war for independence from 1961 to 1974 and then a long civil war from 1975 to 2002. The conflict was between two groups that once fought for independence together. The People's Movement for the Liberation of Angola (MPLA) and the National Union for the Total Independence of Angola (UNITA) were two very different groups with leaders that did not get along, but they were united in their fight against Portuguese colonial rule. When their common enemy was gone, however, the two groups fought one another for control of the newly freed country.

MPLA, UNITA, and UNITA's ally the National Liberation Front of Angola (FNLA) all garnered support from different ethnic groups. MPLA was supported by the Ambundu, as well as the populations in cities. UNITA was supported by the Ovimbundu, a central Angolan group, and other tribes in the east. FLNA was supported by the Bakongo, although it soon developed into a pan-Angolan group that advocated nationalism. These three groups would make up the majority of the population of independent Angola.

Within months of the Portuguese leaving the country, MPLA began forcing UNITA and FLNA forces out of provinces those groups had controlled. By October 1975, the group had sole control over eleven of the fifteen provinces, and foreign countries were concerned. South Africa and Zaire (later renamed the Democratic Republic Congo) backed UNITA, sending forces into the south to help it fight back against MPLA. In November of that year, all three groups declared Angola as independent and each established a different capital: MPLA declared the People's Republic of Angola in Luanda,

FNLA declared Ambriz the capital of the Democratic Republic of Angola, and UNITA declared Huambo the capital of the Social Democratic Republic of Angola. Shortly thereafter, UNITA and FNLA allied against MPLA, and over the next two years most foreign troops left the country. Cuban troops remained to support MPLA, and by 1977 the group had control of most of the south, where fighting was concentrated.

In the 1980s, fighting moved north and west, and South Africa intervened once again. During that decade the war also became a proxy battle between the United States (backing UNITA) and the Soviet Union (backing MPLA). The fighting became more intense in 1986, when both the US and the Soviet Union turned their attention more fully to the country and dedicated more resources to the fight. As the decade ended, a cease-fire was signed by both sides that also set up a framework for peace negotiations. But the deal broke down shortly after, when MPLA accused the United States and South Africa of continuing support for UNITA.

During the 1990s, although fighting continued, MPLA worked to govern the country. The state's first elections were held in 1992, although UNITA and its supporters were excluded, according to international observers. Two years later, another cease-fire was signed and quickly collapsed due to mistrust and a lack of oversight. Fighting finally ended in 2002, when both the leader and the vice president of UNITA died within one month of each other. Leadership passed to Paulo Lukamba, who announced that military operations would be stopped. Leadership from both groups came together to sign a final peace agreement, under which UNITA became a formal political party and disarmed its forces. This brought an end the twenty-six-year conflict.

Although the war was over, the aftermath it left in its wake continues to plague Angola. More than four million people were displaced, and the United Nations estimated that the majority did not have access to medical assistance or water. The infant mortality rate, or the percentage of children to die under five years of age, was around 30 percent, and life expectancy was around forty years old. Despite efforts to translate the country's oil wealth into a better quality of life, the country still struggles with authoritarian governance, with security forces moving against dissidents regularly.

Terrorism in Southern Africa

Southern Africa is the only major region on the continent without a significant terrorist presence. With the exception of the Zimbabwean state, as discussed below, terrorist tactics are not used in the region. Most nations in southern Africa are stable, with established borders and broad cooperation among states. South Africa is the power center of the region and has been proactive in establishing means to counter the threat of terrorism. In fact, southern Africa is the only region in which the US State Department's annual report on global terrorism does not identify large-scale terrorist threats.

The US and South Africa are military allies. Here, soldiers of both countries take part in the joint Shared Accord.

But with the rest of Africa seeing more and more terrorist activity, it is possible that terrorism could strike in southern Africa. The region has widespread income inequality, which can provide terrorist organizations a possible base of support as people become disenfranchised and frustrated.

Al-Aqsa Foundation

Although southern Africa does not have a significant terrorist presence, there are organizations in the region that may be linked to groups the international community has designated as terrorist groups. This includes the Al-Aqsa Foundation, which is headquartered in Germany but has offices in South Africa. The group is set up as a charity organization dedicated to raising funds to help the Palestinian people, but the international community and the United States have found evidence that it is supporting Hamas, the ruling party and terrorist organization in the Gaza Strip. The United States has labeled Al-Aqsa a terrorist organization, and sanctions have been put in place to block it from funneling money to Hamas.

Al-Aqsa isn't the only organization in the country with foreign ties. Qibla, which is considered a terrorist organization, was founded in the 1980s to fight apartheid. But the group also has links to Iran and was inspired in part by the Iranian Islamic Revolution. Qibla was affiliated with PAGAD (discussed later in the chapter) but has not carried out terrorist attacks on its own. It is deeply connected to the larger Muslim community in South Africa, having created the umbrella group Islamic Unity Convention to bring the country's Muslim groups together. Although it preaches in favor of an Islamic government and was founded by a leader with ties to radical Islam, the group is not involved directly in politics and has not been found to be planning attacks against the state.

Robert Mugabe, president of Zimbabwe, rules with fear and intimidation, as well as state-sanctioned terrorism.

Zimbabwe

While terrorist groups are well known and frequently discussed in conflict, state terrorism is more obscure. Terrorism is broadly defined as the use of violence and fear to achieve political goals—literally, to terrorize a population into obedience. In that sense, states are just as capable of terrorism as non-state actors, and in some cases they are able to carry out terrorist actions with efficiency and little opposition. This is the case in Zimbabwe, where dictator Robert Mugabe governs with fear and intimidation.

Mugabe came to power as prime minister following independence in 1980, and over the course of the 1980s, he

Nelson Mandela and the ANC

Today, Nelson Mandela and the African National Congress are considered heroes for their fight against apartheid in South Africa. Yet this wasn't always the case. When the African National Congress first became active in South Africa, the group was considered a terrorist organization by the international community. Nelson Mandela, the group's leader and the first president of post-apartheid South Africa, was on the United States terrorist watch list until 2008.

Nelson Mandela rose to power when he founded the ANC's military wing, called uMkhonto we Sizwe. The group carried out guerrilla attacks against the South African government, and Mandela was arrested in 1962 due to his role in the attacks. In addition to the attacks against the government, the ANC's politics landed it on the list of terrorist organizations. During the Cold War, South Africa's apartheid government had supported the United States against the Soviet Union, and as a result Washington saw value in the government holding on to power. The ANC was sympathetic to communism, which made the group an enemy of the US's Ronald Reagan and the UK's Margaret Thatcher. Despite being on the terrorist watch list for most of his life, Mandela went on to be awarded the Nobel Peace Prize, the US Presidential Medal of Freedom, and the Soviet Union's Lenin Peace Prize. The case of Mandela and the ANC highlights how changing political circumstances can change the way we see groups and how those in power shape our understanding of what qualifies as terrorism.

worked to turn Zimbabwe into a one-party, authoritarian state. He brutally crushed rebellion and dissidents, and in 1987, he was named president by a declaration of parliament. By the end of the decade, he had made himself the sole center of power in the country.

Mugabe has always ruled with brute force, using violence against opponents, aid workers, journalists, and civilians. He has been accused of using rape, torture, and **forced disappearance** against his enemies, particularly in the run-up to elections. In 2008, his security forces and militia intimidated and murdered activists, public servants, polling agents, and civic leaders, along with civilians who were believed to be voting for Mugabe's opposition. When he did not win the election, he authorized beatings, sexual violence, and mutilations to intimidate the opposition. As a result, he won the run-off later that year, after which he continued arresting and disappearing his opponents.

The international response to state terrorism is far more limited than the response to non-state actors, like al-Qaeda. To act against a state suspected of using terror against its own people is to enter a war, which is governed far more strictly and is often subject to larger political trends. Violating a state's sovereignty can be justified under Right to Protect, an international norm meant to stop large-scale human rights violations through international intervention. But meeting that threshold is difficult, and states around the world need to agree that a government is committing atrocities that warrant that intervention. As a result, economic sanctions against the government and leaders is one of the most effective tools foreign governments can use against state terror, although it does not guarantee that leaders will step down or change policies.

People Against Gangsterism and Drugs

An exception to the lack of terrorist activity in southern Africa is the vigilante group People Against Gangsterism and Drugs (PAGAD), which was formed in Cape Town, South Africa. PAGAD was founded as a community organization in the early 1990s, and members staged demonstrations against gang activity, organized crime, and the drug trade. But the group soon began carrying out more radical activities, including setting fire to the houses of those involved in the drug trade and killing gang members.

In 1996, the group was responsible for the mob killing of a gang leader, which marked a turning point both in the group's tactics and in how authorities saw it. Before 1996, the police did not oppose the group because of the very real threat gang activity poses to security. But after 1996, it was clear that the group was becoming a threat itself. The group had connections to Islamic groups like Qibla, though it soon began targeting moderate Muslims and clerics who opposed its increasingly violent tactics.

Between 1998 and 2000, the group carried out bombings in Cape Town that targeted civilians. The government moved against the group, arresting its core leadership and effectively bringing its activities to an end. The government also began carrying out more antigang activities, in part to undermine what the group originally rallied support around. Yet the group still exists and sometimes stages marches in Cape Town. Whether the group will resume carrying out attacks again is unknown, although given its high profile it is unlikely that the state would allow it to become as powerful as it once was.

The Threat of Radicalization in Southern Africa

The rise of PAGAD shows how otherwise stable states can be threatened by terrorism and how populations can be radicalized. The process of **radicalization** is still poorly understood, but many believe it begins with a sense of disenfranchisement and alienation from the ruling government. When young men or women feel they are not being represented or are being oppressed by the state, terrorist organizations can present themselves as viable opposition. This is particularly true in situations where there is no other opposition and a sense of helplessness or powerlessness impacts society.

In some cases, such as PAGAD, groups can tap into a popular issue to build a base of support before gradually becoming more radicalized. Southern Africa has a number of issues that could be used to rally the public, including income inequality and unemployment in cities. However, at this time terrorism is not believed to pose an imminent threat in the region, and groups like al-Qaeda have not established wings in southern Africa.

Joint military exercises are key in maintaining peace. Here, the UN and ECOWAS begin a joint ceremony.

6 The Future of War and Terrorism in Africa

Africa has a number of threats that could lead to future conflict, and terrorism is spreading in all but the southern region. On the other hand, the continent is also home to some of the most proactive antiterrorism and conflict-resolution organizations in the world, with almost all states working closely to try to prevent the next crisis.

Ongoing conflict is one of the greatest threats to Africa's security. The continued fighting in CAR, the DRC, Darfur, South Sudan, and Libya all pose serious threats to stability for neighboring states and provide opportunities for terrorist groups to find safe haven. Ending those conflicts and allowing for strong governance and stability to take root is essential to security, as is ensuring that those who are responsible for current unrest are held accountable.

Other states seem poised for unrest, particularly in the case of long-standing authoritarian regimes. In Algeria and Zimbabwe, oppressive governments have long maintained tight control on civil society, and both are ruled by elderly

The African Union was established to help states cooperate, including on issues of war and terrorism.

leaders who have yet to indicate a possible successor. This could create a power struggle in the wake of their deaths, which has the potential to escalate into civil war. In Kenya, underlying ethnic tensions have led to conflict in the past, and unless it is addressed it could erupt again—as it did in 2008.

Terrorism is also spreading across the northern, western, central, and eastern regions, capitalizing on weak governance and conflict to establish strongholds. The spread of ISIS and al-Qaeda has bred competition between the two, which has in turn prompted more attacks on civilians as they attempt to gain superiority over the other. Combatting terrorism is a multifaceted task, including military operations as well as development of rule of law and engaging the public with governance. To do so, governments must be strong, borders must be guarded, and civil society has to be vibrant.

To combat terrorism and prevent large-scale conflicts, African states have joined and established wide-ranging organizations that work to provide coordination opportunities and assistance. Although some are controversial, and their abilities are limited when dealing with conflicts within independent states like Sudan, these groups have been able to help prevent tragedy. In Madagascar, the African Union promoted rule of law during the 2009 political crisis, using possible economic and political isolation as a tool to pressure the government into finding a solution. Counterterrorism efforts have also been successful in Uganda, where the Lord's Resistance Army has been pushed out of its former territory.

Despite limited successes, however, issues like inequality, poor access to resources like water, authoritarian governance, and ethnic tensions continue to threaten the continent. Africa must deal with these issues to help prevent conflict and combat terrorism.

The African Union

The African Union (AU) is one of the largest and most active continental organizations in Africa. All African states are members, with the exception of Morocco, which left the organization in protest over the recognition of the Sahrawi Republic. The AU has a number of committees and councils aimed at heading off conflict and combatting terrorism across the continent.

The AU established a Commission Strategic Plan in 2013, which outlines the goals the AU hopes to achieve between 2014 and 2017. The plan also reaffirmed the group's vision for its role in Africa, saying:

> The work of the Commission is driven by the belief that the African dream of an integrated continent offering secure, decent livelihoods and the free movement of people, goods and services is not only achievable but can be done in a shorter timeframe. Thus there is a new sense of urgency on the need to accelerate concrete actions to realize the African Union vision.
>
> Our overall goal is to accelerate progress towards an integrated, prosperous and inclusive Africa, at peace with itself, playing a dynamic role in the continental and global arena, effectively driven by an accountable, efficient and responsive Commission. Over the four years of the Strategic Plan period, the Commission will seek to accelerate progress towards a stable, peaceful, prosperous and integrated Africa within a good governance environment, while

paying particular attention to women, youth and other marginalized and vulnerable groups. The Commission will work to build a People-centered Union through active communication of the programs of the African Union, the branding of the Union and participation of all stakeholders, including those in the Diaspora, in defining and implementing the African agenda. Priority will also be given to the strengthening of the institutional capacity of the AUC, and enhancing relations with the RECs and other organs, and with strategic and other partners.

The AU was established in 2001, although it was preceded by a similar organization called the Organization of African Unity that was established in 1963. The AU is built around the Assembly of the African Union, a meeting between heads of state and governments at the group's headquarters in Addis Ababa, Ethiopia, that mirrors the United Nations' General Assembly meeting.

One of the main goals of the African Union is to promote peace and security, as well as foster cooperation among member states and protect human rights. These goals make it critical in fighting conflict and terrorism in Africa. The AU has a dedicated African Commission on Human and People's Rights, headquartered in the Gambia, which meets twice a year to discuss human rights concerns and ways to promote better human rights practices among member states.

The AU introduced the African Peace and Security Architecture (APSA) the same year it was established, which is a comprehensive framework for promoting peace. It includes the Peace Fund and a Continental Early Warning System, as well as the Panel of the Wise, a group of five appointed members representing each region of the continent and charged with mediating potential conflicts. In 2013, the AU introduced the APSA Roadmap 2016–2020, which is designed to help member states hit development and security goals ahead of 2020:

> With a focus on concrete activities and strategic objectives, this Roadmap aims at mapping out a way forward to enable the consolidation of gains made, and address the most pressing challenges, so as to make the African Peace and Security Architecture fully functional and operational, and in this way contribute effectively to the maintenance and preservation of peace and security in Africa.
>
> The APSA Roadmap 2016–2020 details the AUC and RECs/RMs joint aims in five strategic priority areas: Conflict prevention (incl. early warning and preventive diplomacy), crisis/conflict management (incl. ASF and mediation), post-conflict reconstruction and peace building, strategic security issues (such as illegal flows of SALW, IEDs, WMD disarmament, counter-terrorism, illicit financial flows as well as transnational organised crime and cyber crime) and coordination and partnerships. In addition, cross-cutting issues are covered by the Roadmap.

The roadmap also highlights the role of conflict in African governance, current threats, and reasons to believe Africa can become more stable in coming years:

> Conflicts have diminished substantially and peace, security and security are on the upswing, although persistent fragility and new security threats, including the drugs trade, terrorism and tensions over borders remain a major concern. Broad gains are been made on the democratic front, with an increasing number of elections that are free and fair.

The Peace and Security Council (PSC) was established in 2004 as a means to promote collective security and ensure that the group has early warning of possible conflicts. The PSC is in charge of prevention and management of conflicts, as well as negotiating resolutions and promoting reconciliation. The fifteen elected members of the PSC are chosen by the full AU Assembly.

The PSC also maintains the African Standby Force (ASF), which can be deployed to head off conflict around the continent. The ASF is made up of civilian and military forces from all member countries, and troops are maintained in each region to ensure conflicts do not escalate.

The AU has been proactive and aggressive in antiterrorism efforts. In 1999, the AU established the Convention on the Prevention and Combating of Terrorism and the AU Counter Terrorism Framework. Under the protocol, member states must criminalize terrorist activity. The framework provides guidelines on extradition, investigations, and legal assistance. In 2004, the AU started the African Centre for the Study and Research of Terrorism and in 2011 developed the African Model Law on Counter Terrorism to help guide state policy on terrorism prevention.

The Economic Community of West African States

The Economic Community of West African States (ECOWAS) was established in 1975 to promote economic cooperation among regional states. The role of the fifteen-member organization has since expanded to include security and defense. A Protocol on Mutual Defense Assistance was signed in 1981, and member states signed a nonaggression pact in 1990, underlining a commitment to regional peace that was established in 1978 and 1981. The Protocol on Mutual Defense Assistance created the Allied Armed Force of the Community, a standby force similar to the AU's ASF.

The group also established Vision 2020, a set of goals for economic and regional development. According to the ECOWAS website, "The ECOWAS Vision 2020 is aimed at setting a clear direction and goal to significantly raise the standard of living of the people through conscious and inclusive programmes that will guarantee a bright future for West Africa and shape the destiny of the region for many years to come."

ECOWAS established the Economic Community of West African States Monitoring Group (ECOMOG) in 1990, during the Liberian Civil War. It has been deployed in Sierra Leone, Guinea-Bissau, and Monrovia, as well as to combat border fighting between Guinea and Liberia. Although controversial, the group was the first intra-African force to be established and has functioned as an interim force to maintain order until the United Nations is able to intervene.

ECOWAS Controversy

ECOWAS has become one of the leading regional organizations in Africa, but the group has been criticized for what many see as significant shortcomings. There has been disagreement among the international community as well as member states about whether or not ECOWAS has been justified in interventions, including its intervention in the Liberian Civil War. Its effectiveness has been called into question, as ECOWAS has not responded to all humanitarian crises or conflicts in a consistent way. For example, the group did not follow through on plans to intervene in Guinea-Liberia border fighting, and the United States had to pressure it into becoming involved during the Second Liberian War. When it has sent in forces, those troops have been accused of looting and corruption by civilians. In Liberia, the Economic Community of West African States Monitoring Group (ECOMOG)—which is an armed force of ECOWAS—was mocked as standing for "Every Car or Movable Object Gone" in response to thefts by troops.

Bureau of Counterterrorism

The United States has been very active in fighting terrorism in Africa, attempting to head off the spread of terrorism and working to push back terrorist groups' gains. International programs include Countering the Financing of Terrorism, which works to block financial resources for terrorist organizations, and the Foreign Emergency Support Team, which is deployed to assist post-terrorist-attack countries. The Global Counterterrorism Forum is also active in Africa.

There are also Africa-specific programs. The Trans-Sahara Counterterrorism Partnership (TSCTP) is an initiative established in 2005. There are eleven states participating in the program, from across northern and western Africa. Efforts

American soldiers help train soldiers in Sierra Leone to use new weaponry.

are focused on both forming long-term policies to fight the spread of terrorist organizations and providing immediate response to possible threats. The multipronged approach includes training law enforcement in member states, assisting militaries, monitoring borders, and cutting off financial resources for terrorist groups. The TSCTP is also proactive about working with isolated groups that may be vulnerable to extremism to support employment, governance, and access to medical and educational services.

The Partnership for Regional East Africa Counterterrorism (PREACT) has similar aims. It is funded by the US and is focused on comprehensive antiterrorism action. PREACT focuses on promoting justice and the rule of law as a means to fight radicalization, as well as making operations difficult for terrorist networks.

The Global Counterterrorism Forum

The Global Counterterrorism Forum (GCTF) is a large-scale international organization that works closely with the United Nations to combat the spread of terrorism. Algeria, Egypt, Morocco, Nigeria, and South Africa are all founding members, and the African Union works with the organization.

Rather than focusing on military solutions to terrorist threats, the GCTF seeks to combat radicalization, recruitment, and the ideology that encourages terrorism to flourish. The group also focuses on developing civilian capabilities in each member state to help address the needs of communities that are vulnerable to extremism. To do so, the GCTF holds workshops and educational opportunities for member states, as well as provides forums where best practices can be developed and encouraged.

The GCTF has two African-specific working groups. The Horn of Africa Capacity Building Working Group (HOA)

Organization of
Islamic Cooperation

The Organization of Islamic Cooperation (OIC) is an international group established in 1969 to promote solidarity among Muslim nations. Of the OIC's fifty-seven member states, twenty-seven are in Africa, ranging from Algeria in the north to Comoros in the south. Not all are Muslim-majority states, but all of them have a significant Muslim population. The group is dedicated to promoting human rights and security, as well as to fostering communication and cooperation among member states. Given the role of Islamist terror in Africa, the presence of the group is important even if its effectiveness is often called into question.

Since being founded, the OIC has been plagued by controversy and accusations of bias. Outside organizations see it as too hesitant to call out poor practices and support for terrorism among member states, while competing interests have effectively paralyzed it on most issues. The OIC introduced the Convention on Combating International Terrorism in 1999, but many feel the protocol is too vague and defines terrorism too broadly to be effective. The group is mired in politics, making it difficult for it to pass effective resolutions. The OIC identifies terrorism as an ideological issue rather than a security issue, which is an oversimplification but not entirely false. While largely seen as ineffective, the group has been present in CAR, sending a special envoy to assist in mediation between warring factions. The group has also been outspoken in regard to the Libyan conflict, although it has not taken action to help resolve the conflict.

works to help regional states counter terrorist-financing operations, carry out investigations and prosecution, and stop foreign fighters from coming to the region. It also coordinates between regional states to strengthen border security, holds workshops to help develop strategies, and brings experts to the region to help strengthen policy.

The Sahel Region Capacity Building Working Group (Sahel) encompasses a wide territory focused on the Sahara Desert and stretching across the entire continent. It has five priorities, including promoting justice among member states, strengthening borders, cutting off financial resources for terrorist organizations, engaging the community, and working with local law enforcement. It also coordinates regional cooperation and builds support among governments for best practices.

Africa's Future

War and conflict have been part of Africa's recent history, but the continent is also poised to gain stability in the coming years. States across Africa are experiencing economic booms, gains in education, and technological revolutions that are making life better for the average citizen. Because of these fast-moving changes across Africa, the future could be one of peace. But the continent is also home to terrorism, ethnic tension, and a legacy of violence, all of which must be met head on if Africa is going to live up to its vast and incredible potential. Addressing those issues will not be easy for leaders and citizens across the continent, but if done smartly and with dynamic solutions, Africa will benefit immensely, and the people of states across the continent will be able to enjoy safety, security, and prosperity.

Regional Map
of Africa

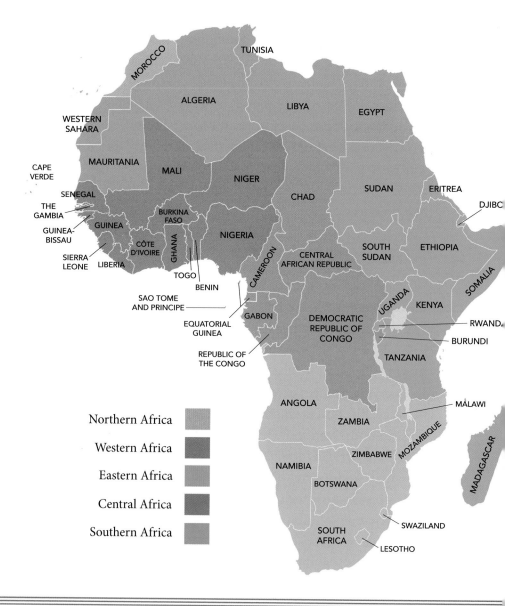

MOROCCO

TUNISIA

ALGERIA

LIBYA

EGYPT

WESTERN
SAHARA

CAPE
VERDE

MAURITANIA

MALI

NIGER

SUDAN

ERITREA

DJIBC

SENEGAL

THE
GAMBIA

CHAD

GUINEA-
BISSAU

GUINEA

BURKINA
FASO

NIGERIA

SIERRA
LEONE

LIBERIA

CÔTE
D'IVOIRE

GHANA

CAMEROON

SOUTH
SUDAN

ETHIOPIA

SOMALIA

TOGO

BENIN

CENTRAL
AFRICAN REPUBLIC

SAO TOME
AND PRINCIPE

EQUATORIAL
GUINEA

GABON

UGANDA

KENYA

DEMOCRATIC
REPUBLIC OF
CONGO

RWAND

REPUBLIC OF
THE CONGO

BURUNDI

TANZANIA

ANGOLA

MALAWI

ZAMBIA

Northern Africa

Western Africa

Eastern Africa

Central Africa

Southern Africa

ZIMBABWE

MOZAMBIQUE

MADAGASCAR

NAMIBIA

BOTSWANA

SWAZILAND

SOUTH
AFRICA

LESOTHO

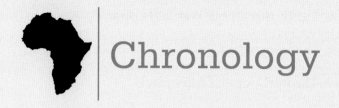

Chronology

1871–1912 The Scramble for Africa results in most of the continent becoming European colonies

1928 The Muslim Brotherhood is founded in Egypt

1956–1975 African states become independent from European colonizing powers

1961 South Africa's ANC becomes militant; Nelson Mandela is arrested

1970 The Western Sahara Conflict begins

1979 The Somalia-Ethiopia War takes place

1980 The LRA is formed in Uganda

1989 President Omar al-Bashir comes to power in Sudan

1989–2003 The Liberian Civil War takes place

1990 Namibia becomes independent from South Africa

1991 Apartheid ends in South Africa

1991–2002 The Sierra Leone Civil War takes place

1991–2002 The Algerian Civil War takes place

1993 Eritrea becomes independent from Ethiopia

1994 The Rwandan Genocide occurs

1994–2005 The Burundi Civil War takes place

1997–2003 The Congolese Civil Wars take place

1999–2003 The Ituri Conflict takes place

2000 The Ivory Coast Civil War breaks out

2001 The conflict in northern Nigeria begins

2002 The Maghreb Insurgency begins; Boko Haram emerges in Nigeria

2004 The Central African Republic Bush War begins

2005–2010 The civil war in Chad takes place

2008 Elections in Kenya spark riots

2009 The political crisis in Madagascar leads to upheaval

2011 Arab Spring protests sweep northern Africa

2012 The Northern Mali Conflict begins

2014 Boko Haram kidnaps two hundred Nigerian schoolgirls

2016 Protests in favor of electoral reforms turn deadly in Kenya

Glossary

annex To take control of a territory and add it to a country's existing territory.

apartheid The legal system of racial segregation that existed in South Africa until 1994.

Arab Spring A series of protests across Arab countries in 2011 that unseated several rulers in northern Africa. The first took place in Tunisia, with protests in Egypt and Libya occurring soon after.

authoritarian A descriptor of a form of government where power is held by one person or small group, and there are few political freedoms.

autonomy Self-government.

cleric A religious leader.

coalition Alliance between separate groups with similar goals.

core al-Qaeda The senior group of al-Qaeda leadership, to which other groups pledge allegiance.

coup The sudden and illegal overthrow of an existing government, usually resulting in the group responsible for the coup taking power for itself.

dissent Sharing opinions or thoughts outside of the norm or unshared by those in power.

ethnic cleansing Killing a population based on its ethnic identity.

forced disappearance When the state uses its power to make an opponent or enemy vanish, often without warning; in most instances such a disappearance means an individual has been executed.

genocide The purposeful targeted killing of a large number of people, usually of one ethnic or religious group.

guerrilla A nontraditional combatant who uses so-called irregular fighting to attack a larger army. Guerrilla armies are usually smaller, not in uniform, and difficult to identify.

humanitarian crisis Any event that is believed to pose a threat to the safety of a large group of people.

insurgency An uprising against the state, attempting to overthrow the government.

interim government A temporary and transitional government.

Islamist group Extremist organization seeking to reorder society according to its interpretation of Islamic law.

Maghreb An area in northwestern Africa centered around the northern Sahara Desert.

marginalize To keep separate from power and authority.

militia Small groups of armed fighters, sometimes loyal to the government and other times opposed to the government.

nomadic Describes populations that do not have permanent settlements and move around in one area.

non-state actors Powerful and influential individuals or groups that exist outside of the government. They can be terrorist groups but are not necessarily aggressive or hostile.

paramilitary Describes fighting forces that are structured and trained like a traditional military but are not considered official armed forces.

police state When a state is controlled through a politicized police force that closely watches the public.

power vacuum When there is no leader or authority, creating a gap in leadership that others fight to fill.

radicalization The process of adopting extremist ideology; the way in which people are recruited by groups like ISIS.

rebellion When a group resists the authority of the government and demands reforms or a change in leadership.

reconciliation The process of healing a community after violence, war, or other traumatic events.

repression The forceful subduing of certain political thoughts, actions, or ideologies by the state.

sectarianism Tension or conflict between branches of the same religion or group, such as the Sunni-Shia conflict in Islam.

stalemate When both sides of a conflict cannot gain ground or the upper hand but fighting continues.

uncontested election An election in which no one argued with or formally complained about the results.

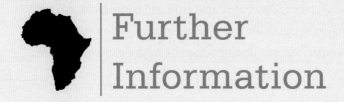

Further Information

Books

Dabashi, Hamid. *The Arab Spring: The End of Postcolonialism.* New York, NY: Zed Books, 2012.

Dowden, Richard. *Africa: Altered States, Ordinary Miracles.* New York, NY: Perseus, 2009.

Mandela, Nelson. *Long Walk to Freedom.* New York, NY: Back Bay Books, 1995.

Meredith, Martin. *The Fate of Africa.* London, UK: Simon & Schuster, 2011.

Reader, John. *Africa: A Biography of the Continent.* New York, NY: Alfred A. Knopf, 1998.

Websites

The African Union

http://www.au/int/

The African Union is a continent-wide organization assisting cooperation and development among member states. All African states, except for Morocco, are members in the group, which meets regularly and issues statements from the continent as a whole.

The Council on Foreign Relations

http://www.cfr.org/projects/world/africa-program/pr1031

A leading Washington, DC, think tank, the Council of Foreign Relations' Africa Program hosts roundtables, publishes studies, and maintains a website featuring analysis on political developments and conflict on the continent. CFR profiles individuals and groups and studies governance and security in the region.

The United States State Department

http://www.un.org/en/sections/where-we-work/Africa/index .html

The United States State Department publishes a yearly report on all terrorist activity around the world, highlighting all current threats, recent attacks, and actions being taken to combat terrorism. Its resources on Africa discuss the most active groups in each region.

Bibliography

Autesserre, Severine. *Peaceland: Conflict Resolution and the Everyday Politics of International Intervention*. New York, NY: Cambridge University Press, 2014.

Baca, Michael W. "My Land, not Your Land." *Foreign Affairs*, August 21, 2015. https://www.foreignaffairs.com/articles/2015-08-21/my-land-not-your-land.

BBC News. "Zimbabwe Rolls out Z$100tr Note." January 16, 2009. http://news.bbc.co.uk/2/hi/africa/7832601.stm.

Blair, Edmund. "Kenya Tourist Numbers Down by a Quarter so Far in 2015." Reuters UK, June 12, 2015. http://uk.reuters.com/article/uk-kenya-tourism-idUKKBN0OS0P520150612.

Bourne, Richard. *Nigeria: A New History of a Turbulent Century*. London, UK: Zed Books, 2015.

Bowker, Tom, Simon Kamm, and Aurelio Sambo. "Mozambique's Invisible Civil War." *Foreign Policy*, May 6, 2016. http://foreignpolicy.com/2016/05/06/mozambiques-invisible-civil-war-renamo-frelimo-dhlakama-nyusi/.

Byman, Daniel. "ISIS Goes Global." *Foreign Affairs*. Retrieved July 10, 2016. https://www.foreignaffairs.com/articles/middle-east/isis-goes-global.

Carayannis, Tatiana, and Louisa Lombard. *Making Sense of the Central African Republic*. London, UK: Zed Books, 2015.

CIFOR. "The Formalisation of Artisanal Mining in the Democratic Republic of the Congo and Rwanda." May 15, 2013. http://www.cifor.org/fileadmin/subsites/proformal/PDF/RIPIS1212.pdf.

Deibert, Michael. *The Democratic Republic of Congo: Between Hope and Despair*. New York, NY: Zed Books, 2013.

Dennis, Anita K., and Benjamin G. Dennis. *Slaves to Racism: An Unbroken Chain from America to Liberia*. New York, NY: Algora Pub., 2008.

Domonoske, Camila. "Morocco Unveils a Massive Solar Power Plant in the Sahara." NPR, February 4, 2016. http://www.npr.org/sections/thetwo-way/2016/02/04/465568055/morocco-unveils-a-massive-solar-power-plant-in-the-sahara.

Driscoll, David. "The IMF and the World Bank: How Do They Differ?" International Monetary Fund. Retrieved May 11, 2016. https://www.imf.org/external/pubs/ft/exrp/differ/differ.htm.

Economist. "An Awakening Giant." February 6, 2014. http://www.economist.com/news/middle-east-and-africa/21595949-if-africas-economies-are-take-africans-will-have-start-making-lot.

Economist. "On and On, They Fight." March 11, 1999. http://www.economist.com/node/319343.

Fraihat, Ibrahimi. *Unfinished Revolutions: Yemen, Libya, and Tunisia After the Arab Spring.* New Haven, CT: Yale University Press, 2016.

French, Howard W. *A Continent for the Taking: The Tragedy and Hope of Africa.* New York, NY: Random House, 2005.

Gold, Zack, and Elissa Miller. "Egypt's Theory of Terrorism." *Foreign Affairs*, June 16, 2016. https://www.foreignaffairs .com/articles/egypt/2016-06-16/egypts-theory-terrorism.

Gourevitch, Philip. "The Life After." *New Yorker*, May 4, 2009. http://www.newyorker.com/magazine/2009/05/04/the-life -after.

Lemarchand, Rene. *Burundi: Ethnic Conflict and Genocide.* New York, NY: Cambridge University Press, 1995.

Mamdani, Mahmood. *When Victims Become Killers: Colonialism, Nativism, and the Genocide in Rwanda.* Princeton, NJ: Princeton University Press, 2002.

McCormick, Ty. "One Day, We Will Start a Big War." *Foreign Policy*, October 28, 2015. http://foreignpolicy. com/2015/10/28/one-day-we-will-start-a-big-war-central- african-republic-un-violence/.

Meredith, Martin. *The State of Africa: A History of the Continent Since Independence.* London, UK: Simon & Schuster, 2013.

Meservey, Joshua. "Somalia's Governance Problem." *Foreign Affairs*, May 15, 2016. https://www.foreignaffairs.com/ articles/somalia/2016-05-15/somalias-governance- problem.

Natsios, Andrew S. "Lords of the Tribes." *Foreign Affairs*, June 13, 2016. https://www.foreignaffairs.com/articles/ sudan/2015-07-09/lords-tribes.

Osman, Tarek. *Egypt on the Brink: From Nasser to the Muslim Brotherhood*. New Haven, CT: Yale University Press, 2013.

Prunier, Gerard. *Africa's World War*. New York, NY: Oxford University Press, 2009.

Stearns, Jason. *Dancing in the Glory of Monsters: The Collapse of the Congo and the Great War of Africa*. New York, NY: Perseus Books, 2012.

Straus, Scott. *Making and Unmaking Nations: War, Leadership, and Genocide in Modern Africa*. Ithaca, NY: Cornell University Press, 2015.

Williams, Paul. *War & Conflict in Africa*. Cambridge, UK: Polity Press, 2016.

Index

Page numbers in **boldface** are illustrations. Entries in **boldface** are glossary terms.

About the Author

Bridey Heing is a writer and book critic based in Washington, DC. She holds degrees in political science and international affairs from DePaul University and Washington University in Saint Louis. Her areas of focus are comparative politics and Iranian politics. Her master's thesis explores the evolution of populist politics and democracy in Iran since 1900. She has written about Iranian affairs, women's rights, and art and politics for publications like the *Economist*, *Hyperallergic*, and the *Establishment*. She also writes about literature and film. She enjoys traveling, reading, and exploring Washington's many museums.